LIMITED
PARTNERSHIPS

How To Profit in the Secondary Market

Richard Wollack
Brent R. Donaldson

Dearborn
Financial Publishing, Inc.

While a great deal of care has been taken to provide accurate and current information, the ideas, suggestions, general principles and conclusions presented in this text are subject to local, state and federal laws and regulations, court cases and any revisions of same. The reader is thus urged to consult legal counsel regarding any points of law—this publication should not be used as a substitute for competent legal advice.

Publisher: Kathleen A. Welton
Acquisitions Editor: Patrick J. Hogan
Associate Editor: Karen A. Christensen
Senior Project Editor: Jack L. Kiburz
Interior Design: Lucy Jenkins
Cover Design: Mary Kushmir

Published by Dearborn Financial Publishing, Inc.

Printed in the United States of America

92 93 94 10 9 8 7 6 5 4 3 2 1

Library of Congress Cataloging-in-Publication Data

Wollack, Richard G., 1945—
    Limited partnerships : how to profit in the secondary market /
Richard Wollack and Brent Donaldson.
        p. cm.
    Includes index.
      ISBN 0-79310-147-6
      1. Mutual funds. 2. Limited partnership. I. Donaldson, Brent.
   II. Title. III. Title: Secondary market.
   HG4530.W65   1992   92-19130
   332.63'27—dc20   CIP

ACKNOWLEDGMENTS

We wish to acknowledge the invaluable help of the following people in preparation of this book:

Sarah Bulgatz
Patti Mervak
John Kramer
John Buckley
Mike Malouf

and a special thanks to James Miller for helping us pull together the diversity of material into a cohesive and intelligent whole.

TABLE OF CONTENTS

LIST OF FIGURES

PREFACE

HOW TO USE THIS BOOK

This book is intended for the growing community of people involved in the limited partnership secondary market—limited partners, active investors, investment analysts, brokers, financial planners and securities firms specializing in the market, as well as researchers, regulators and legislators. It is the first comprehensive overview of this relatively new market. We look at the history of the market, its structure, its dynamics and key issues being debated and addressed today that will shape the market's future.

For the investor, we have attempted to provide enough information about pricing, evaluation and investment strategies so one can intelligently consider potential investments.

For the limited partner seeking liquidity in the market, we discuss the pros and cons of selling into the market and provide a realistic view of what to expect for marketable partnership interests.

Brokers, financial planners and investment advisors should appreciate our in-depth look at partnership structures and evaluation techniques, as well as our comprehensive listings of securities firms active in the market.

For the researchers, regulators and legislators in trade associations and state or federal regulatory and legislative bodies, we have attempted to give an evenhanded review of what we believe are the key issues that need to be addressed in shaping the market's future.

Our viewpoint, of course, has been shaped by our own experiences. We know the secondary market for limited partnerships intimately, having participated in its birth and helping to nurture it through its infancy. We care deeply about its successful maturation into a fair and efficient market that offers limited partners good value for their interests, and offers investors a wide range of opportunities.

Our goal has been to provide enough detail to make this book truly helpful to investment professionals and investors alike, yet to keep our treatment of numerous topics brief and focused. Although we are not attempting to provide legal advice, we have attempted to summarize the legal and technical aspects of investing. However, the partnership secondary market is still fast evolving, particularly in legal and regulatory matters. Hence, any investor should consult with legal counsel in tax and securities matters of partnership market investing. We hope we have provided valuable insights into all key areas of this market.

Dick Wollack
Brent Donaldson
Emeryville, California
May 1992

Open Letter to Brokers and Financial Planners

Many brokers and financial planners who *should* know about the secondary market for limited partnerships simply are not knowledgeable about it, through no fault of their own. Because the market is relatively new and not very well publicized, its functions and features simply are not part of standard broker training or continuing education.

Why should a broker and financial planner know about the secondary market and use it in his or her practice? The reason is that it can offer substantial benefits to many investors, over and above many alternatives.

WHY IT PAYS TO UNDERSTAND HOW CLIENTS CAN SELL THEIR PARTNERSHIPS IN THE SECONDARY MARKET

It is important to know about the market on behalf of your clients who are owners of partnerships they may have purchased in the seventies or eighties. The most common reasons why the secondary market can suddenly become important to such clients are the three "D"s—death, divorce and disability. Often a client or a client's estate has no choice but to liquidate assets, and you need to be able to advise them on how to do so efficiently while commanding the best possible price for their assets.

The fourth "D" is disenchantment. Many investors have become disenchanted with the partnership units they were sold in the seventies or eighties. The broker or planner who sold them the units may no longer be in the business, leaving the investor without means to determine the value of their partnership investment. Many investors tire of late K-1s, excess accounting costs, and may wish to change their investment strategy, if only they knew how to liquidate their partnership.

Brokers should realize that the established dealer firms in the secondary market can be a tremendous ally to themselves and their clients. The firms offer a host of information to educate clients, so brokers can help their clients make an informed decision about sell options.

So if a client groans about K-1s or mentions not getting the returns he or she anticipated or wishes to get out of a partnership, you can get an evaluation from one or more dealer firms. They specialize in pricing partnerships and will generally provide an evaluation, with no obligation, so you can learn what it's worth in the current secondary partnership market. This information will help clients make an informed decision about what to do with a partnership asset.

WHY IT PAYS TO UNDERSTAND HOW TO INVEST IN THE LIMITED PARTNERSHIP SECONDARY MARKET

Brokers or planners with any involvement in the new issue partnership market owe it to themselves to look at the secondary partnership market. In the secondary market, you can buy the same asset class at a maturity of one to ten years from the original issue, at a discount from break-up value and often for less than par (the original offering price). So if you or your clients are looking at the new issue partnership market, you may do better in the secondary market.

From the perspective of efficient markets, the secondary market for limited partnerships is still inefficient. A limited number of buyers have the time, talent and energy to scrupulously analyze and evaluate, and there's a large number of potential sellers. This inefficiency makes it possible for buyers to carefully pick and choose only those partnerships that have the best values for their investment.

Often you can buy units, whether individually or in a pooled fund, where after all transaction costs, you own assets worth more than the original investment. In a new issue partnership, a $10,000 investment may buy you $8,000 of assets after commissions and organizational expenses. In the secondary market, a $10,000 investment may buy you $12,000 or $13,000 of assets after all expenses.

Not only is the pricing more favorable, you also eliminate some of the problems of illiquidity. If it's liquid enough to buy on the secondary market today, two years from now it's likely to be liquid enough to sell. Further, in the secondary market, you eliminate some of the downside of later having to liquidate. You may still take a loss, but it will be nowhere near as great as if you were selling units purchased for full price at the original issue.

And then there's the issue of proven performance. Secondary markets are one of the few businesses where you can have hindsight going into an investment, because you can see how an asset has actually performed. This gives you a tremendous advantage over investing in blind-pool new issue partnerships, where the assets have yet to be specified.

Moreover, there is no down time for investment capital. Your client's money goes right to work because you're buying operational assets. For the same reason, the secondary market investment has a substantially shorter hold period than a new issue purchase.

All these factors add up to safety that is simply not available in the new issue market. By buying known, operating assets at a discount from break-up value, with established performance, better liquidity and shorter holding period, your clients are making a safer, more prudent investment than many comparable alternatives.

INTRODUCTION

We all know what a food market is—it's where we can go to buy the food we need. At the same time, it's a place where people who grow or process food can sell it. New markets evolve as society develops and changes. We have had food markets since humans started cultivating food, but the world market for steel came into being only in the last century. The market for baseball cards didn't exist until the first decades of this century, when enterprising individuals realized that likenesses of Honus Wagner could be sold to burgeoning numbers of baseball fans. Similarly, markets for computer chips and airline frequent-flyer miles have sprung into being in recent years.

How does a new market come into being? It happens whenever two sides of the basic sales equation for any commodity—supply and demand—reach significant enough proportions for buyers and sellers to desire regular exchanges, record keeping and, most importantly, the opportunity to compare and contrast quality, quantity and price out of necessity, the early origins of any new market are informal, but as the volume of trade grows, rules, regulations and conventions evolve. Buyers and sellers alike benefit from having common units of measurement, universally recognized quality standards and agreed-upon trading rules.

Another characteristic of a new market is that there are often tremendous opportunities for "early birds." Imagine that a new commodity becomes available, one that will produce predictable future income over a number of years. Many people who own this commodity have current needs that cannot be met with future income, so they would prefer to sell it for immediate cash. In the early stages of the market for this commodity, there are few buyers, because it is not widely known that the commodity is available, nor is it widely known how to harness its income potential. The few early buyers active in this market cannot absorb all of the supply, so they pick and choose carefully and achieve good value for their investment.

Sellers, of course, are under no obligation to sell. Those who choose to do so are pleased to be able to convert the commodity they own into immediate cash, even if the amount of cash they receive is less than the full potential income stream of the commodity. Thus, both buyers and sellers achieve significant benefits that would otherwise be unavailable to them without the existence of the evolving market for the commodity.

Do such evolving markets with significant opportunity to achieve good investment value exist today? Of course they do, but new markets characteristically are not widely known and understood. Such is the secondary market for limited partnerships—also called the partnership resale market—a relatively new investment arena offering significant opportunities that did not exist just a few years ago. Compared to stocks or bonds, this market is quite small, yet it is growing at a significant rate and seems likely to continue to grow over the next few years. It is at a stage where it has several years' history and has achieved some stability and track record, but a significant portion of its growth curve still lies ahead. It is not a market for everyone, but it holds great opportunity for knowledgeable, long-term investors.

Investors in this market should be knowledgeable because the assets bought and sold—interests in real estate, oil and gas, cable TV and other forms of limited partnerships that have been issued since the early 1970s—are a relatively sophisticated form of investment. They should be long-term investors because the assets will often take years to mature. The sellers are the original investors in limited partnerships who, for whatever reason, do not want to wait out the full term of the investment. They wish to convert their current interest—which may have another 5, 10, 15 or more years to run until its full benefits have been paid out—to immediate cash. Buyers are willing to pay cash for these long-term future benefits.

In 1980, coauthor Dick Wollack was in his tenth year of serving as a general and cogeneral partner for several real estate limited partnerships. Aware that the occasional, but inevitable, liquidity needs of limited partners weren't being met, he realized that providing real liquidity options would not only serve the limited partners, but also could simultaneously sow a new field of investment opportunity. Thus it was in 1980 that Liquidity Fund was formed with Dick Wollack as its chairman and coauthor Brent Donaldson as its president. At its origin, Liquidity Fund pooled investor funds to purchase limited partnership interests as a long-term investment and was the first firm developed specifically to provide liquidity for limited partnership interests. Later, the company pioneered the idea of offering market-making activity similar to that conducted for other publicly offered (corporate) securities. Thus, Liquidity Fund played a significant role in the inception and in the development of a secondary marketplace for partnership interests, a growing market that today meets limited partners' liquidity needs and offers thousands of investors an opportunity for alternative investment options.

We have written this book to help investors and financial advisors understand this new market. We have been active in the market since its inception in the early eighties, have observed its development from its first transactions and care deeply about its future. In one sense, its future is inevitable. As the market continues to grow, it will become more regulated and standardized, which, in turn, will attract more buyers and sellers. But we hope we can increase the rate at which regulation and standardization is developed.

The market already provides great benefits to investors by offering them liquidity for assets they would otherwise be locked into for many years. It provides great investment opportunities to buyers. However, we believe both buyers and sellers will achieve better values by accelerating the standardization process. Thus, we have set out to describe the development of this market in some detail, to explain its structure and dynamics, to identify who the significant players are, to give our analysis of the key regulatory issues and to offer what we feel are well-founded predictions about its future. If we help investors, brokers, financial advisors, legislators and regulators understand this market and thereby facilitate its development to some degree, then we will have achieved our goal in producing this book.

CHAPTER 1

A New Investment Arena

The investing public and the brokers who serve them are only gradually becoming familiar with the secondary market for limited partnership interests. The partnership secondary market is young, with its origins in the early 1980s. It hasn't yet been widely publicized, so many investors aren't even aware of its existence. Others who have heard of it simply don't know how it works.

Public lack of familiarity with the secondary market is understandable. The market is still quite small compared to the stock and bond markets, for example. Its estimated total dollar volume in all of 1991 was some $350 million in trades, roughly 5 percent of the daily total dollar volume of trades on the New York Stock Exchange during the same year.

Nonetheless, brokers, financial advisors and serious investors should understand this rapidly growing market because of the unique investment opportunities it offers. Simply put, interests in seasoned partnerships with track records of a year or more can compare quite favorably with other avenues of investing in real estate, equipment, oil and gas or cable TV.

More specifically, it is vitally important for the eight million to ten million Americans who have invested some $132 billion in limited partnerships since the seventies to understand the partnership resale market. For many such investors, it offers liquidity for their partnership interests that otherwise would be unavailable.

MARKET HISTORY

The market, in a manner similar to the trading of "over the counter" (OTC) stocks, provides the means for investors to buy and sell existing, currently owned units of limited partnership interest. As with OTC trading, there is no specific physical location, such as the stock market's New York Stock Exchange, at which trading takes place. Rather, interests in limited partnerships are traded among a loose affiliation of brokerage firms and specialized dealers. These firms facilitate trade in limited partnership interests because of investor demand for them to do so. To understand how this investor demand developed, we need to look briefly at the history and philosophy of limited partnership investing.

The compelling concept behind syndicated limited partnerships is that they offer average middle-income to upper-income investors an accessible and uncomplicated way to enjoy co-ownership of a pool of assets, without any of the responsibility of managing them. By definition, limited partnerships have traditionally been illiquid investments, designed to be held for the long term. They are created by a "sponsor" or general partner—a firm that makes an initial offering of units to the public and then oversees all facets of the partnership's ongoing management, obtaining fees in payment for its services. Where limited partners' liability in the partnership is limited to the amount of their capital investment, the general partners, entrusted with conducting the partnership's day-to-day operations and guarding the fiduciary interests of the limiteds, are at risk for any uninsured liabilities incurred by the partnership.

Limited liability is a plus of partnership investing, but lack of liquidity is a minus. As an owner of stocks or bonds, it is easy to convert your holdings to cash and put the money to other uses, if your finances, investment strategy or family circumstances change. However, converting a limited partnership interest to cash is inherently more problematic for a number of reasons, including the complexity of accurately establishing current value, difficulty in finding ready buyers, and considerable paperwork and procedural approvals.

A public limited partnership formed in the late seventies through the mid-eighties would typically raise from $50 million to $200 million from many thousands of investors contributing an average of $10,000 each, with minimum investments as low as $2,000. Private limited partnerships, also called private placements, were typically limited to fewer than 100 investors of substantial net worth (referred to as "accredited" investors in the lexicon of securities law—essentially millionaires). They often required an initial investment of $50,000 to $100,000.

In the early eighties, limited partnership investing took off, for a combination of reasons. The stock market was performing poorly (as it had for nearly a decade), and double-digit inflation made the possibility of leveraged appreciation in real estate look very attractive. This drove real estate prices up, which in turn made it even more appealing. The energy crisis created strong interest in oil and gas limited partnerships. Significant changes in tax law, as a result of the Tax Reform Act of 1981, also played a key role in fostering the growth of the limited partnership market. Accelerated depreciation offered significant tax benefits to real estate investors, and the advent of IRAs created a pool of savings that had to be invested for a long term. The nearly $5 billion in interests issued in 1980 rose to some $18 billion issued in 1984. The public invested more than $120 billion in limited partnerships from 1980 to 1990, and has invested more than $132 billion all told (see Figure 1.1). With rising numbers of limited partnership investors, greater amounts of capital invested, and the passage of years during which more people's circumstances changed, the illiquidity of this substantial amount of investment capital became an increasingly significant problem.

Origins of the Partnership Resale Market

During the early seventies, limited partnership investing was still a new concept. Relatively few partnerships existed, and, therefore, the number of limited partners seeking liquidity seemed insignificant. Sponsored partnership investments gained in popularity during the mid- to late seventies and experienced phenomenal growth in the early eighties. With the vastly increased numbers of limited partner investors, it soon became clear that, regardless of an investor's original objectives or the

FIGURE 1.1 Nontraded Partnership Capital Raised, 1970–1990*

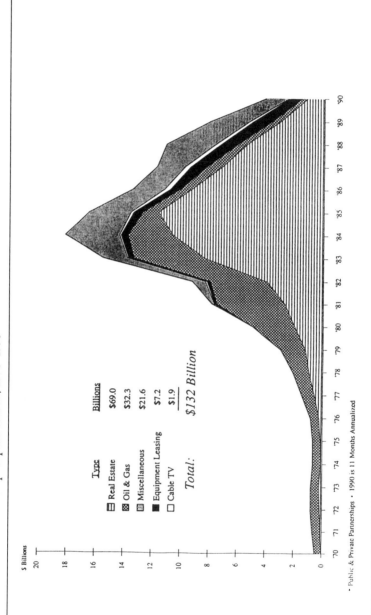

Type	Billions
⊞ Real Estate	$69.0
⊠ Oil & Gas	$32.3
⊞ Miscellaneous	$21.6
■ Equipment Leasing	$7.2
□ Cable TV	$1.9
Total:	*$132 Billion*

* Public & Private Partnerships • 1990 is 11 Months Annualized

SOURCE: Robert A. Stanger & Co., Shrewsbury, New Jersey.

relative health of an individual partnership, there would always be partners who invested with enthusiasm but would later want to get out. By 1980, although the actual percentage of investors demanding liquidity hadn't changed, their numbers had multiplied in absolute terms because of the expanding volume of limited partnerships.

The investor services department of any given partnership sponsor could always expect a certain number of phone calls from limited partners seeking a way to get out. Virtually all partnerships didn't provide for buying back units, so in many cases, the investors were stuck. Some sponsors and general partners offered listing services for interested buyers and sellers, but since the general partners wouldn't receive any compensation for the transfer of units, they had no inherent motivation to effect the transactions—especially with any modicum of speed—beyond their general obligation to serve in the best interests of the limited partners.

In 1980, enterprising entrepreneurs established the first firm dedicated solely to buying investment interests in limited partnerships from sellers who wanted to liquidate their holdings. That move came in response to increasing pent-up demand for a more effective way to provide liquidity for the small percentage of investors who needed it. Today, more than 20 firms specialize in this market as principals or brokers, and the volume of trade, estimated at $350 million in 1991, has been rising some 15 to 20 percent per year.

The first partnerships traded in the secondary market were in real estate, although the market has since expanded to include partnerships in other asset categories: primarily, equipment leasing, oil and gas, and cable TV. As much as the market has grown, however, the bulk of trading continues to focus on real estate, simply because there are greater numbers of real estate partnerships than of any other partnership type. The majority of secondary market transactions involve public partnerships that are operationally healthy, with positive cash flow and substantial equity value. No viable trading market exists for partnerships that are troubled or for those that don't disclose adequate information. Private partnerships typically do not trade because so many of them were designed to generate tax benefits (losses) rather than sound economic results. Further, it's difficult to analyze the viability of private partnerships because information about their performance isn't readily available to the public.

Since 1970, when limited partnerships began to take root, more than half of the approximately $132 billion of partnership securities issued have been in real estate. (See Figure 1.1.) Approximately ten million limited partners now exist in the United States, according to a study prepared by Greenspan Associates for the Investment Program Association. Just a small portion of partnership interests are sold on the secondary market. The 35,000 transfers estimated to have occurred between independent buyers and sellers in 1991 represent a scant one-quarter of 1 percent turnover of all limited partners nationwide. Of course, this annual percentage can vary widely within an individual partnership or within certain asset categories of partnerships, but, overall, the secondary market has room to expand as more investors become aware of its existence. A key reason why such a small volume of limited partners trade their units is that they're unaware of their options and lack information about the secondary market.

Sellers Who Need Liquidity

When an individual contemplates investing in a partnership, the broker selling the securities gives the investor a prospectus that outlines all the limited partnership's terms, investment objectives, financial considerations and risk factors. Although in theory the prospectus is uniquely written for each partnership, it invariably contains some "boilerplate"—language that gets lifted from prospectus to prospectus and recycled over and over again. The description of liquidity serves as a perfect example. The following is excerpted from a prospectus describing the risk factors involved in a real estate offering made in 1984:

> Holders of interest may not be able to liquidate their investment in the event of emergency or for any other reason because (a) presently there is no public market for interests and it is not anticipated that one will develop, (b) the transferability of interests is subject to certain restrictive limitations, and (c) the sale or transfer of interests may result in substantial adverse federal income tax consequences. Such

factors will also limit the price which a holder of interests would be able to obtain for interests.

It's hardly surprising that so few investors know about the secondary market when sponsors seem to deny its existence! The cautious language is understandable, however, since a market for interests in a particular partnership may never develop if its economic performance is sub-par.

This lack of awareness is unfortunate because the market offers substantial opportunities for buyers and sellers alike. For the seller, the after-market provides an escape hatch—a means to liquify an otherwise illiquid limited partnership investment that, for any number of reasons, may have become cumbersome or unprofitable to the investor. Several common reasons for seeking liquidity include:

- a death, birth, marriage or divorce;
- personal financial circumstances requiring cash;
- a desire to get out of an investment no longer yielding its original tax benefits;
- a change in financial planning goals;
- tax preparation costs and headaches; and
- a better opportunity elsewhere to make a more attractive alternative investment.

Opportunities for Buyers

For the buyer, the market represents an opportunity to purchase a proven, mature investment at a discount from current value. By offering cash at a time when the seller needs it, the buyer provides an important benefit to the seller, which is why the seller is willing to relinquish his or her holding at a substantial discount.

Two avenues are available to buyers who wish to participate in the partnership after-market: (1) as an individual or (2) as a limited partner in a pooled fund dedicated to investing in the partnership secondary market. One can invest as an individual through a broker or financial planner by: first researching the existing operational partnerships owning assets in a particular category of interest (e.g., real estate, oil and gas, equipment leasing or cable TV); analyzing the partnerships' prior performance record and financial statements to assess current and potential value; and then making a purchase of pre-owned units based on this individual appraisal of value. This route is taken by some sophisticated investors with substantial assets to commit.

Alternatively, a buyer can invest as a limited partner in a pooled fund investing exclusively in pre-owned units selected from among a diversified group of limited partnerships. Similar in concept and design to mutual funds, these pre-owned partnership funds provide an effective way for the average investor to participate in a managed portfolio of growth-oriented or income-oriented securities without having to perform the preliminary research and analysis necessary to evaluate the assets and, similarly, without having to worry about paperwork or administrative tasks. Many investors choose this pooled investment approach because it allows them to avoid the initial and ongoing administrative cost burden of purchasing a portfolio of securities on their own.

Trading in partnership interests has attracted a number of more active investors. In this case, the investor will select and purchase partnership interests directly, hold them briefly, then resell them to long-term investors.

WHY INVEST IN THE SECONDARY MARKET?

For an investor, purchasing pre-owned units can yield substantial advantages over purchasing a new partnership issue.

- The secondary market buyer, whether an individual or a pooled fund, has a *clear picture* of what will actually be in the investment. Unlike blind-pool partnership investments—into which investors sink their capital before the partnership's assets have even been specified—the pre-owned units represent interests in an existing portfolio of assets that is much closer in time to realizing their ultimate investment goals. The units, in essence, have already been "seasoned." That is, the partnerships have already survived and prospered through the riskiest time of any investment—the start-up. They have already yielded tangible investment results in the form of current cash distributions and/or equity appreciation.

- A buyer in the secondary market can *better predict* what type of distributions, and overall yield, he or she can expect from the investment and can also calculate whether current distributions come from real earnings or merely from the partnership's cash reserves.
- The assets have a *shorter holding period*, resulting in an earlier realization of capital growth. Because the existing partnerships are further along in their life cycle than newly issued units, the buyer enters an investment often having a much more compressed time line.
- Buyers have a *wide choice* in the types of partnership units they can purchase. Whether they want current income, capital growth or some combination of the two, they can select the type of investment that will best accommodate their goals.
- Some investors can use the partnership secondary market to adjust or *fine-tune the tax effects* produced by their overall investment portfolio. For example, investors may have excess passive income or losses from other investments. To balance these excesses, they can acquire the exact type of partnership units they need to produce the appropriate offsetting benefit.
- Purchasing pre-owned units *doesn't involve the payment of any "front-end" organizational fees* as do most purchases of new (i.e., primary) issues. These fees, which can be substantial, can dilute the equity of new-issue units by 20 percent or more. This means that an investor making an initial investment of $10,000 in a new issue may be able to purchase only $8,000 in assets after deducting the front-end fees and commissions required by the sponsor or general partner. Conversely, when an investor puts $10,000 into the secondary market, he or she can typically acquire at least $10,000 of actual equity, even after all costs of the transaction are deducted.
- Overall, the purchase of a pre-owned unit *reduces uncertainty* and investment risk, compared to the purchase of a newly issued partnership unit.

The overriding benefit, however, is the *discount from net asset value* (also referred to as "break-up" value), at which units are typically acquired. We shall take a detailed look at the reasons behind such discounts in Chapter 5. For now, it is sufficient to understand that the enhanced equity position possible in secondary market investing translates into greater overall investment returns for the buyer.

KEY MARKET PLAYERS

Five types of services meet various needs of investors in the secondary market:

1. Listing services
2. Electronic bulletin board
3. Agents or riskless principals
4. Dealers
5. Pooled investment funds

These services differ substantially in the roles they play in effecting trades, the extent of services offered and the risk they are willing to assume on behalf of investors. (See Figure 1.2.)

Listing Services

General partners. A few general partners provide nominal listing services for limited partners who wish to trade units. They develop and maintain internal lists of interested buyers and sellers for a particular limited partnership. Upon request, they will provide a prospective seller with a copy of the list of buyers, or they will give an interested buyer the list of sellers. When a buyer and seller decide to make a transaction, they inform the general partners, who then complete the transfer at the next designated transfer date before forwarding the sales proceeds to the seller. Very few general partners record transfers in their books on a daily basis; more do it monthly, but the great majority transfer units only once a quarter. Thus, a seller who wants or needs cash right away may find that it takes quite a long time to get it.

Broker-dealers. Certain brokerage firms, particularly large New York Stock Exchange firms who have sold a lot of original

FIGURE 1.2 Secondary Market Participants

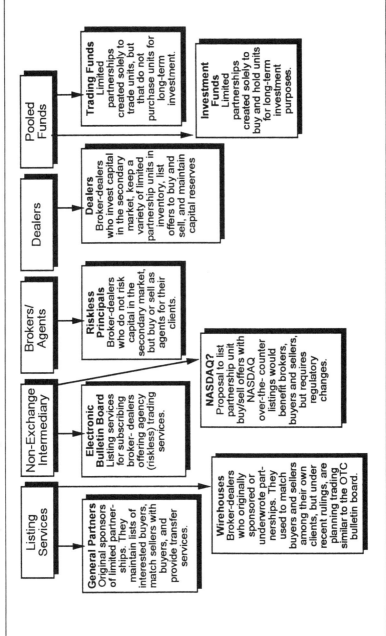

issue limited partnerships, formerly provided listing services. These wirehouse listing services were historically responsible for more than one-half of the dollar volume of partnership units traded, and tended to be managed more actively than those maintained by general partners. At the time of this printing, these firms' trading activity has been suspended pending review of an SEC pronouncement preventing any issuer (or its affiliate) from "making a market" in its own securities without filing an ongoing registration with the SEC. It appears that these difficulties will be resolved and NYSE firms with affiliated GPs will reopen their trading desks but in a manner consistent with SEC rules and regulations.

Electronic Bulletin Board Exchange

In 1985 a subscription service, the National Partnership Exchange (NAPEX), was formed that is available only to registered broker-dealers. It lists trading partnerships and attempts to match buyers and sellers. A seller who wants to liquidate units in a limited partnership lists them through a subscribing broker or financial planner at a specific offering price. Brokers from subscribing firms place bids on the offering, creating competition among potential buyers. NAPEX charges both the buyer and seller a commission. They may also face a stock brokerage fee for the services provided by their broker or financial planner.

NAPEX assumes no risk in the transactions that occur; it pays the seller only after a transfer has been recorded by the general partner and after NAPEX has received written confirmation. Thus, like listing services, NAPEX does not provide immediate liquidity in the secondary market for limited partners who wish to sell right away.

Agents

Some brokerage firms will act as agents or "riskless principals" in facilitating secondary market trades. These firms refer prospective sellers to dealers or other brokers or financial planners that represent a buyer. Occasionally, the agent may conduct some of the negotiations on behalf of the seller and may process the paperwork involved. In other cases, a firm does not permit its representatives to take commissions on secondary market transactions, so their services are minimal.

Dealers

Dealer firms are responsible for about one-half of all the partnership units traded. For a number of reasons, dealers are in a better position to offer services to buyers and sellers, compared to the listing services offered by wirehouses, general partners or the electronic bulletin board. For one, they are independent, not associated in any way with the sponsors of the partnerships they trade. Another essential difference is that they present offers to buy and sell limited partnership interests for their own account, rather than merely acting as an agent. Because dealers buy and sell the assets themselves and own an inventory of many of the more commonly traded partnership units, they can offer two-sided quotations (on the buy or sell side) to brokers or financial planners who make inquiries on behalf of clients. Some larger dealer firms, in addition to creating a wholesale market for trades between brokerage firms, also conduct direct retail-level transactions with sellers and buyers.

The greatest advantage dealers offer sellers is that they customarily pay for the units right away, before transfer of ownership is necessarily recorded by the general partner. In addition, the dealer often guarantees that the buyer of the units will receive partnership distributions after a specified date, even though the actual transfer of ownership (and appropriate "record date" for distributions) may not yet have occurred and the general partner may continue to send distributions to the seller.

Pooled Investment Funds

Individuals who want to invest in the partnership secondary market can do so on their own using a broker/financial planner or a dealer to effect their trades. Or they can invest in a pooled fund—a limited partnership that invests exclusively in pre-owned partnership units. Some of these funds purchase and hold units as long-term investments. Others function as "trading" funds, which actively and continuously buy and sell.

THE FUTURE OF THE PARTNERSHIP
RESALE MARKET

The partnership secondary market is an emerging market, still in need of consistent rules to help shape its sustained growth and success. Before it can function like other securities markets, it must become more widely recognized and understood by the public and by the securities industry; the volume of trading must increase; standardized settlement, transfer and distribution procedures must be determined; and consistent quotation and transaction data must become more easily accessible.

Nonetheless, the market already provides a significant alternative to limited partnership illiquidity for those investors who need it. As public awareness of the market increases, and as sponsors and general partners take a greater role in maintaining it, the services it offers can only improve. There are a number of clear signs that this is occurring, such as increasing cooperation between dealer firms, an improved understanding of the market by regulatory agencies and legislators, and the proposal or implementation of specific legislation and regulations designed to protect investors and improve the efficiency of the market.

The market is likely to grow substantially into the mid-nineties for three reasons. First, more original issue partnerships will become mature enough to attract buyer interest, so the supply will increase. Second, many marginal partnerships will work through their difficulties as economic recovery and progress of the real estate cycle combine to improve conditions in troubled markets, which will further increase the supply of investment-grade secondary units. But we believe the greatest impact on market growth will be more readily accessible information about pricing and about the market itself. As more partnerships qualify for the trading universe, far greater numbers of buyers, sellers, brokers and financial planners will be aware of how it works and how to take advantage of it.

CHAPTER 2

Selling Limited Partnership Units

Limited partners who sell their partnership units may wish to convert their investment interest into cash for a variety of reasons. Investors who opt to sell do so with the understanding that the price they receive will typically represent a discount from the units' "break-up value" or "net asset value"—the amount paid per unit if all of a partnership's assets were sold at current market rates, all of its liabilities were paid off and its remaining cash were distributed to the limited partners. Thus, the decision to sell isn't, and shouldn't be, made lightly. Rather, it results from careful consideration of all the available alternatives.

REASONS FOR SELLING

What leads limited partners to the decision to sell their units? In most cases, their financial circumstances have changed over time. The limited partner who invested in a partnership in 1983 has different financial needs and objectives in 1992.

Another significant factor is the performance of the national real estate and oil and gas markets over the past decade. Many limited partnerships formed in the mid-seventies were designed to exist for five to ten years but have had their lives extended to 15 years to 20 years. Others issued in the eighties have no immediate end in sight. Postponing property sales has been a common strategy for real estate partnerships in particular, many of whose assets have wallowed in a slow-growth or no-growth phase because of slack economic conditions in those markets where the partnerships bought properties.

In many of these cases, it appears that the partnerships would have been better off waiting to sell the assets until local market conditions had improved and prices had climbed enough to make property sales economically viable. The general partners had extended the partnerships' lives in the belief that, given enough time, they would have been better able to realize the assets' upside potential.

Extending the life of a partnership beyond the original "marketing and sales story" is well within the realm of a general partner's options. Most prospectuses provide for the partnership's life to be extended to as long as 30 years or 40 years, given adverse conditions. Some investors may not have focused on this possibility, considering an extension unlikely based on the sponsor's track record with other partnerships that had successfully completed their investment cycles within their specified time frames.

Whether or not an investor is in an extended-life partnership, there typically are significant personal conditions contributing to a decision to sell. Who are the limited partners who choose to sell? If they knew when they invested that they would be locked in to the investment for a minimum of five years, and maybe as long as ten, what suddenly motivates them to sell? When an investor finds that buyers are not willing to pay the full potential break-up value of their units, but will buy them only at a substantial discount, what circumstances impel them to sell the units anyway? Below we describe some of the most common reasons for deciding to liquidate limited partnership units prior to the completion of the full partnership life cycle.

Upon retirement, an investor wants to redeploy assets into a more liquid investment with more current income. Consider, for example, an individual who invested in a growth-oriented real estate partnership in 1980, believing he or she will be cashed out by 1990. Getting the initial investment back plus capital gains at that time would have coincided with the investor's retirement in early 1992, allowing him or her to roll over the principal into an income-oriented investment that would better serve the investor's changed financial needs. However, an extension of the partnership's asset holding period creates a problem that may be best addressed in the secondary market.

As another example, consider an investor in a leveraged-asset partnership who is facing an early, unexpected retirement. The partnership, though performing well, is designed only for capital growth. While the investor's need for current income has suddenly swelled, the sale of the partnership's portfolio is still a long way off, and current distributions from operations are minimal at best.

A tax-exempt investment plan is about to dissolve. Pension plans have their own life cycles. The trustees may have included limited partnership investments in the plan's portfolio in order to reap the rewards of equity appreciation, under the assumption that the partnerships' assets would come to fruition and be sold by a specific date. Now the plan itself may be about to dissolve, but the partnerships still have no clear end in sight. Cash is needed to pay out to the plan's beneficiaries.

A couple needs to fund a child's education. A couple may have counted on receiving back the capital in their partnership investment by a certain date in order to finance their child's education. Extending the partnership's life now means that the cash won't be available to them when they need it.

An investor dies. The estate frequently needs to liquidate long-term investments in order to pay inheritance taxes and distribute assets.

An individual inherits an unwanted investment. Many partnership investments are held by estates. Often, the beneficiaries of these estates have no need for or interest in retaining the partnership units, since the partnership doesn't match their tax or financial planning needs or their investment objectives.

An unexpected, unbudgeted event occurs. A business reversal may create a sudden need for cash, or an uninsured loss or uninsured medical expense may have created a sudden debt.

A spouse or other income provider dies. The death of a spouse, or a divorce, can create a need for a different kind of investment with current income and more liquidity.

Fluctuating market conditions have rattled an investor's interest in continuing to own certain types of assets. Many people who invested in oil and gas in the early eighties, for example, believed that world oil prices would be substantially higher today than they actually are. They no longer have faith that their investment will yield the income they originally hoped for and want to get out in order to reinvest something they believe will work out better for them.

An investor wants to restructure his or her asset portfolio. Because of changing financial goals, a limited partner may choose to reapportion his investment portfolio to strike a different balance between the asset types he or she owns. The investor may decide that he or she should have less capital tied up in real estate, for example, and more invested in government bonds.

An investor has more income and a larger investment portfolio than when he originally went into the partnership. Some people simply no longer need the partnership for retirement or long-term savings purposes. They want to liquidate units in order to purchase a new car, a new or second home, or to finance a special vacation or special event, such as a wedding.

Tax laws have changed. During the seventies and early to mid-eighties, significant tax benefits were a primary consideration for many individuals who invested in public and private partnerships. Tax benefits, economic performance aside, would make the investment worthwhile. In most cases, limited partners enjoyed substantial write-offs from these investments from accelerated depreciation of the assets and from the generation of initial net operating losses. However, the 1986 Tax Reform Act, by restricting the deductibility of passive tax losses, dealt a harsh blow to those who came to rely on limited partnerships as a vehicle for tax shelter. In phased steps, the new rules increasingly limited the use of passive losses so that they could be applied only to offset income that was, likewise, passively earned.

The tax incentives behind limited partnership investing were such a strong investment incentive that, after 1986, fund-raising for partnerships of all types fell off substantially. Many of the limited partners who had invested prior to 1986 were content to stay with their investments. Others, for whom the primary reason to invest was the promise of a tax shelter, have sought a way out, since they no longer can fully utilize the tax benefits.

* *Partnership tax reporting is a big headache.* The 1986 tax reform and the 1987 Tax Act not only took away tax benefits, but also complicated the preparation and increased the cost of annual income tax returns for investors. To add insult to injury, the measures also limited the deductibility of fees associated with tax preparation. Tax accountants estimate that adding a limited partnership investment to an otherwise routine tax return can increase the time and cost of preparing the return by some 20 percent to 30 percent. Some accountants impose a fee for each K-1 partnership return a client has.

According to estimates of the Investment Program Association, the syndication industry's trade group of general partners, more than one-half of the ten million limited partners in the United States regularly seek income tax filing extensions because of their untimely receipt of Schedule K-1 information from partnership sponsors. These delays, coupled with the bigger headache of more complicated, higher cost tax returns, have convinced many individuals to sell their partnership units in favor of simpler investments.

An investor feels uncomfortable with owning a limited partnership. Many individuals invested on the advice of a broker or adviser without giving any real consideration to the nature of the investment. Even though the partnership may now be generating healthy distributions or otherwise be performing in accordance with its original investment objectives, these limited partners may feel uncomfortable owning the units. Perhaps they've read a lot of negative press about the downturn in real estate, or they just can't make sense of the financial statements they receive each quarter. They also may feel insecure because the partnership no longer has a definite "ending" date. To them, their partnership investment represents more of a risk than anything else, and they would like to get rid of it in favor of another investment that's simpler and easier to understand.

Fear of a limited partnership "rollup" sparks the desire to sell. A now widely condemned practice of combining (or restructuring a single) partnership into one entity that gets traded on a securities exchange began in the early eighties. "Rollups" often unfairly overcompensated their organizers and usually resulted in devaluing the limited partners' interests. The trend was substantially slowed in 1990 and 1991 by bad publicity, resistance from investors and new regulations. Also called "mergers," "restructurings" or "reorganizations," roll-ups effectively cost limited partners billions of dollars in lost equity during their heyday. Many partnership interests entered the secondary market because limited partners feared that their units might get "rolled up" and lose value. The danger of roll-ups has diminished over the past year or so and is likely to disappear entirely with the passage of federal legislation. Nonetheless, this phenomenon was a significant factor in the partnership secondary market in the mid-eighties. Chapter 5 has a more detailed analysis of the effects of roll-ups on limited partners and on trading in the secondary partnership market.

A limited partner finds a better investment.   An investor may encounter an opportunity that looks attractive, but that requires an amount of cash that he or she doesn't have. Upon careful analysis, the limited partner may find that even after the discount for selling the partnership units, the alternative investment offers better prospects for a higher return.

Whatever the motivation, investors who sell their limited partnership interests have decided they do not want to wait several years for the partnership to complete its cycle and liquidate its portfolio to realize the assets' full value. Instead, it is more important to have cash in hand today, even at a substantial discount from the current break-up value of the underlying assets.

After listing so many reasons that commonly provide such motivation to sell, it's important to note that few limited partners choose to do so. Only a small percentage of investors (less than 1 percent per year) sell their units. In part, this is due to the fact that the secondary market for partnership interests isn't widely known, but, even more significantly, it is because the vast majority of limited partners have no desire to get out of their partnerships.

Selling Partnerships: A Case Study

To help understand more clearly how a typical secondary market transaction can fit with the specifics of a family's financial situation, let's look in detail at the circumstances of a hypothetical family, the Jacksons.

Bill and Betty Jackson of Ashland, Oregon, have been married for 20 years and have a son, 15, and a daughter, 17, who are entering their freshman and senior years in high school, respectively. Bill manages a lumber mill and his wife owns a small shop. They own their home and have a combined annual income averaging $65,000, which enables them to live comfortably, but doesn't allow them to set aside much for savings. Their income is high enough, however, to make them ineligible for any significant financial aid when their children start college.

Inherited partnerships. Bill's father, in the course of saving for his retirement, had acquired a diverse portfolio of assets that included small investments in certificates of deposit, mutual funds, individual stocks, and government bonds, as well as sizable interests in four different limited partnerships. In 1990, only two years after Bill's mother had passed away, Mr. Jackson, Sr., died, leaving his entire estate to Bill, his only son.

The limited partnership investments Bill's father made in 1981 were the most significant component of the estate, representing a total of $100,000 in original contributed capital ($25,000 in each partnership). (See Figure 2.1.)

FIGURE 2.1 The Jacksons' Four Partnerships

Partnership	Investment Type	Investment Goal	Yield	Capital Gains	Overall Performance
Income Realty, Inc.	All cash real estate	Maximum current income	Averaged 8% over life of partnership; currently at 8%	Capital gains on sale of properties	Distributions over life of partnership to date have paid back original investment
Realty Growth Associates	Moderately leveraged real estate	Maximum equity appreciation compatible with modest income	Has fallen from 5.5% to current 3%	Capital gains on sale of property	Moderately leveraged real estate diversified by type and area awaiting overall real estate market turnaround for maximum performance
Equipment Masters, Ltd.	Equipment leasing	High income with equity growth from reinvestment of excess cash flow	10% for last 5 years	Repayment of invested capital on liquidation of equipment	Income has been excellent. Overall performance depends on final value of assets on disposition.
Cable Communi-cations Fund I	Purchase of existing cable TV franchises	Equity growth	0%	Substantial capital gains on sale of cable franchises	Rapid growth of cable franchise subscriber bases promises excellent overall return.

The first, Income Realty, Ltd., was a real estate partnership that purchased income properties for cash. Its primary investment objective was to maximize current income from property operations to support the highest level of consistent, quarterly distributions to limited partners. The second partnership, Realty Growth Associates, was also a real estate partnership, but, unlike Income Realty, Ltd., was structured to purchase properties using as little cash and as much leverage (financing) as possible in order to maximize the opportunity for equity appreciation. Also, unlike the income-oriented real estate partnership, this one provided minimal current distributions to partners. The third partnership investment was in Equipment Masters, Ltd., an equipment leasing entity that made all-cash purchases of marine cargo containers, truck trailer units, double stack rail cars and other related shipping equipment that were leased to transportation companies. The partnership's goal was to offer investors high current income with some capital growth possible. Finally, the fourth partnership was Cable Communications Fund I, a program that franchised the start-up and operation of several local cable providers in the Pacific Northwest.

Over the years, Income Realty, Ltd. had performed well, generating regular quarterly distributions at the rate of 8 percent per annum. By 1992, just before his death, Mr. Jackson, Sr., had received back the bulk of his original investment in distributions from the properties' cash flow alone. Eventually, when the assets are sold, the partnership would also generate substantial capital gains from the equity appreciation. Equipment Masters, Ltd., had also performed well, producing distributions regularly with each year of operations averaging about 10 percent. The Cable Communications Fund I program hadn't been generating any current distributions, but had significantly appreciated in value because of its expanded customer base; it was expected that large capital gains would result when the assets were sold.

On the other end of the performance spectrum, Realty Growth Associates had not fared well. Many of the partnership's properties were office buildings located in Texas and other Sunbelt areas where vacancy rates had been high and market values had sagged. In general, however, Mr. Jackson, Sr., had been pleased with his partnership investments and understood that even though Realty Growth Associates' income statement didn't look very healthy at the moment, the assets held the promise of attractive returns down the road, since market conditions were showing signs of improvement.

A need for cash.   When Bill and Betty inherited the estate, they debated whether they should let the partnership investments mature to maximize the return on investment or see if there was some way they could cash them in to help finance their children's college education. Without some extra cash near term, the children would either have to attend the local community college or would need to take a couple years off to work to help fund their education.

The couple reasoned that if they sold all four partnerships, they could reinvest a portion of the sales proceeds to generate a higher level of current income than they were currently earning from the two income-oriented ones. The combination of higher current income with the principal they would receive might enable them to fund the children's educations at a top private college. Of course, they realized that holding onto the partnerships for the additional five to seven years that it would take for them to liquidate in the normal course of operations would result in a significantly better return, but, on balance, they decided that they needed the money now and that it didn't make economic sense for them to wait.

Finding a buyer.   Once they made the decision to sell, the Jacksons called the general partners of each of their partnerships to find out what their sales options were. In three of the four cases, they met with little success. Representatives of the equipment leasing partnership said, "We're not set up to handle buybacks, but the partnership will only exist for another four or five years before it sells its remaining assets, and we strongly encourage you to wait until that time." The investor services departments of Income Realty, Ltd., and Cable Communications Fund I offered to send them the lists of interested partnership buyers they had on hand, consisting of brokers and dealers that had called the partnerships to express an interest in buying those units and in being included in the lists. The Jacksons requested copies but still wanted to find one central source through which they could sell all their partnership holdings at once.

An investor relations representative at the growth-oriented real estate program was the most helpful. She told the Jacksons that an independent secondary market did in fact exist for limited partnership units and that over a dozen firms handled the transactions and would provide price quotations. She also mentioned three sources of secondary market price information: *The Wall Street Journal's* periodic report on selected partnership resale prices, *Stanger's Investment Advisor* and *Partnership Profiles* (Figure 2.2), which lists recent trading prices for hundreds of different partnerships. Finally, she suggested they might start by calling several partnership secondary market dealers and trying to pin down the best price themselves.

It was clear to the couple that they would need to do quite a bit of investigation before they signed a contract to sell, so they called the broker who originally sold the units to Bill's father to get her advice. She gave them the names and phone numbers of several dealers that could handle the entire transaction for them. She cautioned them that there were considerations over and above the price offered for the units, such as how quickly proceeds would be paid and what fees would be charged against the proceeds, not to mention the stability and track record of the dealer firm. Her point was that each firm tended to have its own idiosyncrasies in pricing, fees and transaction timing, and that their offers had to be compared carefully to determine which would provide them with the best value. Finally, she warned them to expect that all offers would be at a discount, perhaps significantly lower than what they might expect the units to be worth. She explained that although the theoretical "break-up" value of a unit might be, say, $700, if all the partnership assets were sold and liabilities paid off, no buyer would be willing to pay them the full $700, since the buyer would be taking on the burden of waiting for the partnership to mature and the risk of owning an asset which could decline in value.

The Jacksons called several firms to compare price quotations. They discovered that some firms maintained that they could close the transaction and get them a check within five days, while others indicated that the process could take as long as four

FIGURE 2.2   Sample Listings of Limited Partnership Secondary Market Prices

SECONDARY SPECTRUM

PARTNERSHIP	ORIGINAL PRICE	TRADING PRICES HIGH	LOW	CURRENT YIELD
RAI. Yield & Equities III	$1,000	$520	$520	N/A
Rancon Realty Fund III	$1,000	$463	$463	N/A
Rancon Realty Fund IV	$1,000	$588	$475	N/A
Rancon Realty Fund V	$1,000	$550	$522	N/A
Real Equity Partners	$1,000	$432	$200	N/A
Realmark Property Investors LP V	$1,000	$370	$370	N/A
Resources Accrued Mortgage Investors 2	$250	$27	$22	0%
Resources Accrued Mortgage Investors 86	$250	$10.50	$10.50	0%
Resources Pension Shares 5	$10	$2	$1.62	N/A
RWB Medical Income Props. 1	$1,000	$460	$380	N/A
SCA Tax Exempt I	$1,000	$415	$415	N/A
Shelter Properties IV	$1,000	$70	$70	0%
Shurgard Growth Capital 15	$1,000	$532	$532	10.8%
Shurgard Growth Capital 17	$1,000	$570	$417	10.1%
Shurgard Income Properties 14	$1,000	$581	$527	11.9%
Shurgard Income Properties 16	$1,000	$580	$535	11.5%
Shurgard Income Properties 18	$1,000	$616	$485	12.7%
Shurgard Income Properties II	$500	$350	$350	12.1%
Shurgard Income Properties III	$500	$450	$350	10.9%
Shurgard Income Properties IV	$1,000	$630	$630	11.1%
Shurgard Income Properties V	$1,000	$463	$462	12.1%
Shurgard Income Properties VI	$1,000	$544	$544	11.0%
Shurgard Income Properties VII	$1,000	$543	$543	10.6%
Shurgard Income Properties VIII	$1,000	$400	$358	10.6%
Shurgard Income Properties IX	$1,000	$570	$570	11.9%
Shurgard Income Properties X	$1,000	$551	$499	10.3%
Shurgard Income Properties XI	$1,000	$525	$525	11.4%
Shurgard Income Properties XII	$1,000	$550	$460	12.3%
Shurgard Mini-Storage LP I	$500	$375	$375	12.7%
Signature XII Ltd.	$10,000	$6,500	$6,500	N/A
Southmark Equity Partners II	$1	$0.26	$0.26	11.5%
Southmark Equity Partners III	$1	$0.10	$0.10	0%
Summit Insured Equity L.P.	$25	$10.75	$8.60	N/A
Summit Insured Equity L.P. II	$25	$11.50	$8.70	N/A
Summit Tax Exempt II	$20	$9.90	$7	12.3%
Summit Tax Exempt III	$20	$12.15	$8.20	11.8%
Travelers Income Properties I	$1,000	$58	$58	N/A
United Storage Associates 85-I	$1,000	$825	$825	N/A
USAA Income Properties IV	N/A	$285	$285	N/A
Wells Real Estate Fund I	$250	$140	$140	N/A
Westin Hotels LP	$1,000	$350	$210	N/A
Windsor Park Properties 4	$100	$66	$66	8.7%
Windsor Park Properties 5	$100	$75	$75	10.3%
Windsor Park Properties 6	$100	$70	$70	10.4%
Winthrop Partners 81	$500	$274	$274	N/A

EQUIPMENT LEASING PARTNERSHIPS

PARTNERSHIP	ORIGINAL PRICE	TRADING PRICES HIGH	LOW	CURRENT YIELD
Aircraft Income Partners L.P.	$500	$218	$166	26.0%
AIRFUND II International Partners	$25	$9	$9	33.3%
American Income Partners III-A	$25	$9	$9	N/A
American Income Partners III-B	$25	$11	$11	N/A
American Income Partners III-D	$25	$12.56	$12.56	N/A
American Leasing Investors III-C	$500	$135	$135	N/A
American Leasing Investors IV-B	$500	$175	$78	N/A
American Leasing Investors IV-C	$500	$107	$82	N/A
American Leasing Investors V-A	$500	$350	$217	N/A
American Leasing Investors V-B	$500	$370	$220	N/A
American Leasing Investors V-C	$500	$385	$330	N/A
ATEL Cash Distribution Fund III	$10	$9.25	$8.60	N/A
Capital Preferred Yield 1	N/A	$173	$173	N/A
Datronic Equip. Income Fund XVII	$500	$473	$400	N/A
Datronic Equip. Income Fund XVIII	$500	$473	$450	N/A
Datronic Equip. Income Fund XIX	$500	$455	$455	N/A
Fidelity Leasing Income III	$500	$230	$195	N/A
IEA Income Fund VII	$500	$430	$388	30.6%

PARTNERSHIP	ORIGINAL PRICE	TRADING PRICES HIGH	LOW	CURRENT YIELD
IEA Income Fund VIII	$500	$409	$373	20.5%
IEA Income Fund IX	$500	$339	$303	18.7%
IEA Marine Container Fund II	$500	$220	$220	31.8%
IEA Marine Container Inc. Fund III	$500	$286	$260	40.3%
IEA Marine Container Inc. Fund VI	$500	$454	$371	30.3%
Jetstream, L.P.	$20	$11.70	$5.34	23.5%
Jetstream II, L.P.	$20	$11.50	$5.70	25.6%
National Lease Income Fund 3	$500	$173	$38	N/A
National Lease Income Fund 4	$500	$250	$95	N/A
National Lease Income Fund 5	$500	$407	$397	N/A
Pegasus Aircraft Partners	$20	$8	$6	34.3%
Pegasus Aircraft Partners II	$20	$11	$7	22.2%
Phoenix Leasing Income Fund 1981	$1,000	$125	$125	N/A
Phoenix Leasing Cash Dist. Fund III	$250	$183	$138	N/A
PLM Equipment Growth IV	$20	$17.75	$14.55	13.0%
PLM Equipment Growth V	$20	$16.75	$14.55	12.8%
PLM Trans. Equipment VII C 1985	$500	$130	$130	23.1%
PLM Trans. Equipment IX B 1986	$500	$139	$139	32.4%
Polaris Aircraft Income Fund I	$500	$39	$20	0%
Polaris Aircraft Income Fund II	$500	$133	$40	28.9%
Polaris Aircraft Income Fund III	$500	$130	$60	21.1%
Polaris Aircraft Income Fund IV	$500	$259	$141	22.5%
Polaris Aircraft Income Fund V	$500	$350	$231	19.8%
Troy Lease Income LP	$500	$165	$165	N/A
Wellesley Lease Income A	$500	$130	$130	N/A

CABLE TV PARTNERSHIPS

PARTNERSHIP	ORIGINAL PRICE	TRADING PRICES HIGH	LOW	CURRENT YIELD
American Cable TV Investors 2	$500	$825	$770	0%
American Cable TV Investors 3	$500	$715	$516	0%
American Cable TV Investors 4	$500	$405	$278	0%
American Cable TV Investors 5	$500	$367	$186	0%
Cable TV Fund 12 - A	$500	$640	$640	0%
Cable TV Fund 12 - B	$500	$728	$475	0%
Cable TV Fund 12 - C	$500	$600	$500	0%
Cable TV Fund 12 - D	$500	$665	$463	0%
Cable TV Fund 14 - A	$500	$640	$367	0%
Cable TV Fund 14 - B	$500	$335	$300	0%
Cable TV Fund 15 - A	$500	$308	$293	0%
Cencom Cable Income Partners	$1,000	$700	$600	N/A
Cencom Cable Income Partners 2	$1,000	$713	$713	N/A
Enstar Income Program 1984 - 1	$250	$165	$115	0%
Enstar Income Program II - 1	$250	$160	$105	0%
Enstar Income Program II - 2	$250	$160	$105	0%
Enstar Income Program IV - 1	$250	$155	$110	0%
Enstar Income Program IV - 2	$250	$155	$110	0%
Enstar Income Program IV - 3	$250	$155	$100	0%
IDS/Jones Growth Partners 87-A	$250	$135	$135	0%
Jones Cable Income Fund 1 - B	$500	$202	$202	8.9%
Jones Cable Income Fund 1 - C	$500	$400	$315	7.5%
Northland Cable Prop. Five	$500	$500	$420	2.2%
Northland Cable Prop. Seven	$500	$425	$425	2.4%
Northstar Income Fund I	N/A	$227	$181	N/A

OIL & GAS PARTNERSHIPS

PARTNERSHIP	ORIGINAL PRICE	TRADING PRICES HIGH	LOW	CURRENT YIELD
PaineWebber/Geodyne Energy I-B	$1,000	$90	$90	N/A
PaineWebber/Geodyne Energy II-A	$1,000	$43	$34	N/A
PaineWebber/Geodyne Energy II-B	$1,000	$50	$37	N/A
PaineWebber/Geodyne Energy II-D	$1,000	$51	$51	N/A
PaineWebber/Geodyne Energy II-E	$1,000	$50	$50	N/A
PaineWebber/Geodyne Energy III-A	$100	$60	$59	N/A
PaineWebber/Geodyne Instit. Pension Energy Income P-4	N/A	$70	$70	N/A
Parker & Parsley 82-III	N/A	$64	$64	N/A
Parker & Parsley 85-B	$1,000	$200	$200	N/A
Parker & Parsley 88-A	$1,000	$368	$368	N/A

SOURCE: Partnership Profiles, Inc., Dallas, Texas.

FIGURE 2.2   Sample Listings of Limited Partnership Secondary
Market Prices   (continued)

LIMITED PARTNERSHIP
SECONDARY-MARKET PRICES
April 1, 1991 to March 31, 1992

The following table summarizes, by investment category, secondary-market prices for public limited partnerships based on actual transactions during the twelve-month period indicated. Seventeen secondary-market firms provided high and low price data.

The secondary market for limited partnerships is an "informal" market, lacking a centralized trading system. Transaction prices can vary dramatically for any given partnership based on the number of units changing hands and the number of firms active. Therefore, the reported transaction may not reflect current pricing in the secondary market. Partnerships listed may have received return of capital.

Type/Partnership	Original Price Per Unit	Transaction Price Per Unit 12 Mos. Ended 3/31/92 High	Low	Total Units Traded During This Period	Type/Partnership	Original Price Per Unit	Transaction Price Per Unit 12 Mos. Ended 3/31/92 High	Low	Total Units Traded During This Period
REAL ESTATE — EQUITY					**REAL ESTATE — EQUITY** (continued)				
AEI RE 16	$1,000	$ 680.00	$ 612.00	2	Balcor EQPSN 2-TX	$ 250	$ 68.00	$ 32.00	941
AEI RE 17	$1,000	$ 875.00	$ 875.00	15	Balcor EQPSN 3-TX	$ 250	$ 115.50	$ 97.50	92
AEI RE 86-A	$1,000	$ 698.00	$ 698.00	30	Balcor EQPSN 4-TX	$ 250	$ 91.00	$ 84.00	200
AMFAC/JMB Hawaii 1	$1,000	$ 550.00	$ 425.00	245	Balcor Equity 12	$1,000	$ 100.00	$ 100.00	10
Aetna Prop 1	$ 20	$ 10.00	$ 9.00	400	Balcor Equity 18	$1,000	$ 146.00	$ 100.00	191
Aetna RE Assoc	$ 20	$ 11.90	$ 4.75	9,683	Balcor Income 1	$1,000	$ 30.00	$ 30.00	333
Amer Afford Hous 2	$1,000	$ 735.00	$ 735.00	10	Balcor Mobile HIF 1	$ 15	$ 8.99	$ 7.03	18,275
American Ret Villa 1	$1,000	$ 600.00	$ 400.00	107	Balcor Realty 82	$1,000	$ 50.00	$ 25.00	105
American Ret Villa 2	$1,000	$ 675.00	$ 425.00	92	Balcor Realty 83	$1,000	$ 50.00	$ 40.00	50
American TC Prop	$1,000	$ 650.00	$ 650.00	10	Balcor Realty 84	$1,000	$ 45.00	$ 35.00	30
American TC Prop 2	$1,000	$ 752.00	$ 725.00	66	Balcor Realty 84-2	$1,000	$ 95.00	$ 40.00	60
Angeles Inc Prop 1	$ 500	$ 2.00	$ 2.00	40	Balcor Realty 85-1	$1,000	$ 80.00	$ 40.00	145
Angeles Inc Prop 2	$ 500	$ 60.00	$ 20.00	144	Balcor Realty 85-2	$1,000	$ 40.00	$ 27.00	90
Angeles Inc Prop 3	$ 500	$ 140.00	$ 35.00	245	Balcor Realty 85-3	$1,000	$ 40.00	$ 40.00	50
Angeles Inc Prop 4	$ 500	$ 130.00	$ 46.67	1,390	Balcor Realty 86-1	$1,000	$ 40.00	$ 40.00	22
Angeles Inc Prop 5	$1,000	$ 190.00	$ 15.00	318	Boston Cap TC Fund	$ 10	$ 8.00	$ 6.77	6,500
Angeles Inc Prop 6	$1,000	$ 300.00	$ 85.00	315	Boston Cap TC Fund 2	$ 10	$ 8.11	$ 8.11	1,000
Angeles Opportunity	$1,000	$ 530.00	$ 375.00	106	Boston Fin Apt Assoc	$1,000	$ 100.00	$ 100.00	35
Angeles Ptnr 8	$1,000	$ 10.00	$ 10.00	15	Boston Fin QHTC	$1,000	$ 560.00	$ 560.00	25
Angeles Ptnr 9	$1,000	$ 168.00	$ 150.00	10	Boston Fin QHTC 2	$1,000	$ 800.00	$ 550.00	180
Angeles Ptnr 11	$1,000	$ 165.00	$ 100.00	36	Boston Fin QHTC 3	$1,000	$ 700.00	$ 690.00	3,026
Angeles Ptnr 12	$1,000	$ 290.00	$ 163.00	55	Boston Fin QHTC 4	$1,000	$ 747.00	$ 695.00	810
Angeles Ptnr 14	$1,000	$ 90.00	$ 90.00	15	Brauvin High Yield	$ 10	$ 9.00	$ 6.37	3,100
Angeles Ptnr 15	$1,000	$ 458.00	$ 67.10	296	Brauvin High Yield 2	$1,000	$ 850.00	$ 700.00	136
Angeles Ptnr 16	$1,000	$ 554.00	$ 130.00	29	Brauvin Inc Prop 6	$1,000	$ 660.00	$ 610.00	35
Apartment Inc Fund	$ 500	$ 440.00	$ 440.00	20	Brauvin RE Fund 5	$1,000	$ 58.00	$ 58.00	15
Arvida/JMB 1	$1,000	$ 475.00	$ 215.00	994	Budget Storage 1	$ 500	$ 315.00	$ 315.00	50
Arvida/JMB 2	$1,000	$ 500.00	$ 260.00	207	Burger King 1	$1,000	$1,019.00	$ 840.75	65
Balcor Col Stor 85	$ 250	$ 168.00	$ 115.00	5,953	Burger King 2	$1,000	$ 925.00	$ 925.00	40
Balcor Col Stor 86	$ 250	$ 170.00	$ 36.00	1,860	Burger King 3	$1,000	$ 900.00	$ 750.00	148
Balcor Cur Income 85	$1,000	$ 215.00	$ 124.00	269	CNL 2	$ 500	$ 446.00	$ 395.00	127
Balcor EQPSN 1-TE	$ 500	$ 240.00	$ 40.00	2,680	CNL 3	$ 500	$ 463.00	$ 463.00	5
Balcor EQPSN 2-TE	$ 250	$ 125.00	$ 32.00	6,005	CNL 6	$ 500	$ 435.00	$ 410.00	100
Balcor EQPSN 3-TE	$ 250	$ 225.00	$ 72.00	3,858	CPA: 1	$ 500	$ 290.00	$ 250.00	328
Balcor EQPSN 4-TE	$ 250	$ 103.00	$ 55.00	279	CPA: 2	$ 500	$ 648.00	$ 469.00	459
Balcor EQPSN 1-TX	$ 500	$ 160.00	$ 115.00	526	CPA: 3	$ 500	$ 650.00	$ 466.00	908

*Number of secondary market firms reporting trades in the listed partnership during the specified reporting period.

SOURCE: Reprinted with permission from *The Stanger Report*, published by Robert A. Stanger & Co., Shrewsbury, New Jersey.

months. Nonetheless, the range of offers gave them a clear picture that the current market value of their four partnerships would total up to little more than $75,000, compared to the $100,000 Bill's father had invested. With that number in mind, they looked at how they might put the money to use to fund their children's college education.

Even with their children taking out student loans, they estimated that currently, good private colleges would cost them about $12,000 per year out of pocket. They worked out a chart to see how the proceeds from the sale of the partnerships could help them with the cost of college over the next seven years.

In plotting the future costs of college education and how they would meet them, the Jacksons assumed that their out-of-pocket college costs would increase 7.5 percent per year, so that by their son's senior year in college, seven years later, they would have to come up with more than $18,000. They also agreed that they could afford to pay $2,500 out of pocket the first year, and that they would increase that amount by 12 percent each year, paying $2,800 the second year, $3,136 the third year and so on. Finally, they anticipated that four years hence, the year when their son entered college while their daughter was a senior, they would have to pay double costs, or nearly $30,000. (See Figure 2.3.)

In talking with their financial planner, they discovered that they could invest the proceeds from the partnerships in tax-free bonds that would yield 8 percent income. With those figures in mind, they were able to work out a plan for reinvesting the partnership proceeds to provide the liquidity and income they would need to fund their children's education.

Once they worked out the numbers, it was clear to the Jacksons that selling the partnership units would give their children the freedom to attend any college they could get into. They selected a firm called Partnership Liquidity Services, Inc., (PLS) to help them liquidate their partnership units. Although PLS didn't quote the highest prices for all the units and required a minimum fee of $200 to handle the transaction, its bid was among the top three and only a few dollars per unit less than the top price. More importantly, it offered a firm price that wasn't subject to change, it guaranteed closing within two to six weeks, and it would handle every step of the process, from start to finish.

FIGURE 2.3   The Jacksons' College Payment Plan

	Year 1	Year 2	Year 3	Year 4	Year 5	Year 6	Year 7	
1) College Costs	12,000	12,900	13,868	29,815	16,026	17,228	18,520	Total Costs: 120,355
2) Paid from Personal Earnings	2,500	2,650	2,809	2,978	3,156	3,346	3,546	From earnings: 20,985
3) Must Be Paid from Other Sources	9,500	10,250	11,059	26,838	12,869	13,882	14,973	
4) Starting Sale Proceeds ("College Fund")	78,125	74,115	68,974	62,549	38,568	27,755	14,983	
5) Paid from College Fund	9,500	10,250	11,059	26,838	12,869	13,882	14,973	Paid by Fund: 99,371
6) Remaining College Fund	68,625	63,865	57,916	35,711	25,699	13,873	9	
7) Interest Income into College Fund*	5,490	5,109	4,633	2,857	2,056	1,110		
*Invested in 8% tax-free bonds 8) Ending in College Fund	74,115	68,974	62,549	38,568	27,755	14,983		

The Jacksons figure that college costs (line 1), currently at $12,000 per year, will increase 7.5%/year, and they plan for double expenses in Year 4, when both children will be in college.

On their current budget they will pay $2,500 per year from their joint earnings, and figure to increase that amount 6% per year (line 2).

The remaining college expenses must be paid from another source (line 3).

They will place the total proceeds from the sale of their partnerships ($78,125) in a tax free bond fund (line 4), and will pay the rest of the yearly college costs from the fund (line 5).

This leaves a substantial remainder in the fund (line 6) earning interest at 8% tax free (line 7). This interest adds to the principal, increasing the cash available for the next year (line 8). The total amount in the fund at year-end (line 8) becomes the Starting College Fund for the next year (line 4).

Based on these assumptions, college costs for both children will total $120,355 over 7 years.

They will pay $20,985 of this amount from their earnings, and another $99,371 will be paid from the principal and earnings of their partnership proceeds.

Figure 2.4 illustrates the secondary market sales performance of the four partnerships owned by the Jacksons by comparing the units' original offering prices, current net asset values as stated by the general partners, and the partners' remaining capital accounts at the time of sale, with the values assigned to the units by PLS.

Once the Jacksons decided to sell to PLS, their representative called the general partners of each of the four partnerships to verify that the Jacksons were in fact registered owners of the units they said they wanted to sell, and to determine requirements of each partnership regarding signature guarantees or notarizations to effect a transfer of units. Within three days, the Jacksons received separate sales contracts for each of their partnership holdings, along with requests to have their signatures guaranteed or notarized as required. Also required was a copy of Mr. Jackson, Sr.'s, death certificate for each partnership, as proof of transfer of estate ownership. The Jacksons executed the agreements, had their signatures appropriately witnessed and returned all the paperwork to PLS. Four weeks later, they received a check in the amount of $78,925, representing proceeds from all their partnership interests, less the $800 in transaction fees charged by PLS.

Key Variables for Sellers

Getting the best deal in the partnership aftermarket requires attention to three factors: timing, price and service. Different sellers may attribute greater significance to any one of the three, although all should be considered in deciding when, how and where to sell. For example, a particular seller may find that he or she needs to be paid within one week and will thus have to accept a lower price for his or her units in order to achieve his or her timing goal. Another seller may not need cash quite as quickly and, being able to wait for a longer period of time, may be better positioned to obtain a higher price. To some sellers, the best price may be of paramount importance. To others, the best service fulfills a greater need.

FIGURE 2.4 Secondary Market Value of the Jacksons' Partnerships

	Original Price per Unit	Number of Units	1991 Net Asset Value (stated by general partner)	1991 Break-Up Value (determined by market maker)	Secondary market price per unit	Total from secondary market sale of units
Income Realty, Ltd.	$1,000	25	$900	$850	$633	$15,825
Realty Growth Associates	1,000	25	785	700	458	11,450
Lease Masters, Ltd.	1,000	25	1,200	1,200	866	21,650
Cable Communications Fund I	1,000	25	1,900	1,900	1,200	30,000

Total raised from sale of units: $78,925

Transaction fee ($200 per partnership): -800

Net proceeds to Jacksons: $78,125

Timing. An individual who contemplates selling a partnership investment should think about when the best time to sell might be. If the sales price exceeds the seller's tax basis for the units, the seller can realize an ordinary gain representing the difference between the tax basis and the sales price. If, in the current year, the seller had passive tax losses from other investments, this might be an optimal time to sell the units. These losses could offset some or all of the gain from selling the partnership units.

The amount of time it takes to have one's name removed from the partnership's records should be another consideration in choosing when to sell. Because general partners are slow to effect unit transfers on the partnership's books, it could take up to an additional three months for the selling partner's name to be officially removed from the partnership's records after the partner has received a check for the sale. This time lag can represent a problem if the partner's Schedule K-1 then shows tax consequences to the partner for a period of time when he or she no longer owned the units. An adjustment on the partner's tax return will correct this mistake, but the complication can be avoided completely if the partner sells early enough in the year.

Price. Obviously, sellers are most concerned about how they can obtain the best price for their units. Discounts from net asset value in the secondary market vary from firm to firm and from partnership to partnership. Limited partners often forget that their units don't have the same monetary value they had at the time of initial investment. This is particularly true of limited partners whose units are held through custodial accounts and trusts. The trust statements they receive consistently list the units at par value, often because no other generally accepted market value exists, and don't show adjustments for return of capital. Because the investment appears in their statements this way, people are lulled into believing that their investment is simply worth its original cost. The fact of the matter is that, depending on the performance of the partnership, the units could be, and most likely are, worth less or more than what the investor originally paid for them.

It's not easy to do a financial analysis of a partnership portfolio, mainly because of the lack of asset appraisal information that's so essential for accurate valuation. It's for this reason that discount levels tend to vary; each buying firm applies its own appraisal and valuation criteria to the partnership assets being analyzed. Further, buyers make this same calculation and will only offer "so much." Additionally, the secondary market considers only the actual amount of capital, per unit, that the partnership has invested in its asset portfolio. Therefore, any amounts representing "front-end" fees are excluded. In most limited partnerships, these fees reflect the sponsor's compensation and costs in connection with organizing the partnership and raising funds, and they can range from 15 percent to 25 percent of a limited partner's invested capital. That means that, of a $10,000 initial investment, as little as $7,500 may actually have been available for the partner's share of the investment in assets. The seller should be aware of this in evaluating the discount from original par value that is applied to the units.

When obtaining a bid, selling partners must be careful to ask whether the price they are being quoted is "firm." In other words, could there be any reason for the price to change before the deal goes through? Brokers and dealers that buy the units for their own account typically provide a firm, guaranteed price, as will those firms that are effecting a trade and already have a unit buyer lined up. Some firms, however, quote "best efforts" prices that are contingent on their finding a buyer (at those prices). If they can't find a buyer, then they lower the price until one appears.

Dealers may also charge a transaction fee for all of the purchases or unit trades they effect. Recall that in the hypothetical Jackson sale, for example, the flat fee charged by PLS was $200. For a ten-unit investment that originally cost $1,000 per unit, this fee doesn't represent a significant amount. For a limited partner who wants to sell only two $1,000 units, however, the transaction fee would dramatically erode the sales proceeds. Limited partners should consider whether the number of units they have to sell justifies the cost of a sale in the secondary market.

Service. Limited partners need to determine that the firm they select will perform in accordance with their expectations so that the deal they strike won't fall through. In addition to getting a firm price, they should also be able to get a commitment on when the transaction will close.

Reputation. Selling partners should evaluate the reputation and solidity of the firm. Questions to ask are: How long has the firm been in business? Is it in compliance with applicable securities laws? As we'll see in the following chapter, these and other issues are important considerations for buyers as well.

CHAPTER 3

Opportunities for Buyers

The partnership secondary market does more than provide liquidity for limited partners. It also gives new investors the opportunity to find attractive values for their investment dollars with a higher degree of predictability and safety than they would find in the initial offering market for limited partnerships. A number of factors are drawing sophisticated investors to the market, particularly those with a long-term view of the real estate cycle and a liking for unusual opportunity.

THE REAL ESTATE CYCLE

Buyers have various motives for wanting to enter the market, but many with an interest in real estate believe that the real estate cycle is approaching, or has reached, its nadir. At the height of a real estate cycle, after two or three years of fast-rising real estate values in key markets, more and more people want to own real estate. The excess of investment dollars chasing after the same commodity quickly drives prices higher and higher and causes more and more new development, until values are driven far above what long-term, conservative real estate investors are willing to pay. Eventually, the cycle turns down as overbuilding creates high vacancy rates and drives down rents. Investors who own overpriced properties begin to default on their financing, and in many markets both lenders and developers are deeply troubled. As this part of the cycle evolves, the public swiftly loses interest in investing in real estate, buyers are few and far between, new development slows to a standstill and prices stagnate or drop.

Eventually, prices begin to make economic sense again, but few people notice that fact. Most investors wait on the sidelines until much later in the "up" part of the cycle. The end of the eighties and the start of the nineties clearly were a down part of the cycle for many real estate markets. Nationally, apartment starts were estimated to have fallen to 150,000 in 1991, the lowest level since 1956, when about 130,000 apartments units were started, according to real estate economists. This low point was reached even though the average long-term mortgage rate had dropped to 8.87 percent, the lowest rate in 14 years, and the cost of development was relatively low—a further sign that perhaps the bottom of the development cycle had been reached.

The essential question is whether demand is truly increasing. When new construction lags behind increasing rental demand, rents rise, owners of existing real estate increase operating income, developers start more new construction and real estate goes on the upswing. (See Figure 3.1.)

As we move further into the nineties, many experienced, long-term real estate investors are quietly acquiring properties. They want to be owners of real estate as the trend line of slowed development (and thus, limited supply) inevitably is crossed by the countering demand trends of economic recovery and population growth, increasing rental income and asset values. As demand grows in the face of limited supply, prices will rise faster and faster, and those who carefully acquired assets during the "down" part of the cycle will be in a position to increase rents (and the returns on their investments), and sell at a profit.

A PARTNERSHIP EMPORIUM

Thoughtful investors also see an unusual buying opportunity created by the negative press that gave partnerships in general (and real estate partnerships in particular) a bad name in the late eighties. On top of the normal distortion of values caused by the downswing of the real estate cycle, they observe that secondary

FIGURE 3.1 Real Estate Cycle

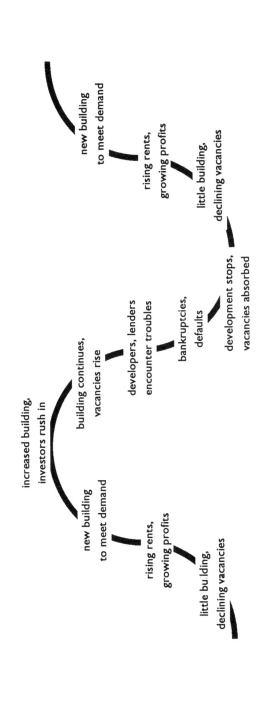

new building
to meet demand

increased building,
investors rush in

building continues,
vacancies rise

developers, lenders
encounter troubles

bankruptcies,
defaults

development stops,
vacancies absorbed

new building
to meet demand

rising rents,
growing profits

little building,
declining vacancies

rising rents,
growing profits

little building,
declining vacancies

market prices for partnership units often are much lower than what actually is justified by the partnerships' economics. For those with some foresight, the secondary market can be like a bargain emporium with few other shoppers. They can wander the aisles, picking and choosing the best values.

How large is this emporium? From 1971 to 1990, approximately $132 billion in limited partnership units were issued, of which $69 billion were in real estate, with the rest distributed among oil and gas, equipment leasing, cable TV and other types of partnerships. In 1990, an estimated $300 million of these partnership units were traded through the secondary market— less than one-quarter of one percent of the total amount issued over the previous twenty years.

The best guess of secondary market experts is that trading topped $350 million in 1991, and that the market is likely to continue to grow at an annual rate of 15 percent to 20 percent for the next four to five years. We discuss the future potential of the market in more detail in Chapter 6, but suffice it to say here that the market definitely is on a growth trend. Currently at a mere one-quarter of 1 percent of the total limited partnership universe, there is plenty of room for the market to double or triple in size. The rewards for buyers have been consistently high. Financial planners and brokers who overlook this new market are missing out on a unique and compelling investment opportunity.

BARGAIN HUNTING IN THE SECONDARY MARKET

Compared to a new-issue partnership, there are many advantages to buying pre-owned partnership units, such as the following:

1. *Proven performance*—the units are backed by seasoned portfolios of assets with actual operating results on which to rely for analysis.
2. *Shorter holding periods*—secondary units have shorter holding periods, having already gone through the organizational and acquisition phases, as well as several years of ownership.

3. *Potential tax benefits*—the investment can be structured to meet and take advantage of specific tax needs.
4. *Low transaction cost*—transaction fees do not have to subsidize the many organizational costs associated with new issues.
5. *Immediate investment returns*—return on investment begins right away because the assets are already "up and running."
6. *Excellent values*—buyers perform an important service by "cashing out" sellers who otherwise would have to wait years to reap the fruits of their investment. Sellers are willing to accept a substantial discount from the actual "break-up" value of their units as a way of compensating buyers for this service.

Such advantages are attracting more and more investors to the secondary market. Let's take a closer look at the actual dynamics of these investment features. (See Figure 3.2.)

Proven Performance

The fact that secondary market partnerships have already acquired their assets and managed them for a few years allows investors to be more certain of obtaining their goal of income or growth than a "blind pool" new-issue partnership with speculative plans about properties it hopes to acquire. Proven performance translates into lower risk. Buying a pre-owned unit means buying into a specified portfolio of seasoned partnership assets. It means you can judge a general partner's actual management performance on the specific assets you will own, rather than having to guess at how they will perform based on their previous track record on other assets. You can look at tangible operating results—an actual income stream, real management expenses, cash in the bank, outstanding loans and liabilities—instead of a marketing department's projections and estimates.

For instance, consider a new-issue real estate limited partnership raising capital from investors with a promise to purchase income properties. Although the limited partners may generally understand that their partnership will build or buy a portfolio of apartment and office buildings, they do not know what or where

FIGURE 3.2   New-Issue Partnerships versus Secondary Market Partnerships

	New-Issue Partnership	Secondary Market Partnership
Management Track Record:	Known from previous partnerships	Known from current partnership
Property Track Record:	Unknown	Documented
Holding Period:	Organizational period plus full term of partnership property hold. Typically 10-15 years.	No organizational period and less than full term of partnership property hold. Typically 5-10 years.
Return on Investment	Waiting period while partnership acquires properties	Begins immediately
Organizational Cost:	Partnership organizational costs amount to 15-25% of investment	None

the buildings will be, much less how well they will ultimately perform. Instead, investors are shown sales and marketing brochures that illustrate the sponsor's past performance. The sales kits invariably contain four-color glossy photographs or flattering artists' renditions of properties that had been acquired for the sponsor's previous partnerships. Naturally, these photographs present the cream of the portfolio's crop. Enticing architectural elements, swimming pools, verdant landscaping, pristine views and evidence of impeccable maintenance are incorporated to appeal to the average investor's own perceptions of "the good life." More than for aesthetic value alone, the photographs and illustrations are selected to highlight properties where the investors themselves would want to live, work or shop.

An individual or couple considering a new partnership investment can be seduced by the story and pictures of the sponsor's past successes and decide to invest. Of course, beside (or beneath) each photograph or artist's rendering a disclaimer points out that the illustration is only representative of the type of property that will be purchased by the partnership and will not in fact be one of the properties to be included in the current partnership's portfolio. The investors, therefore, rely extensively on the sponsor's reputation and their faith in it when they make the decision to write a check. They simply believe and trust that the sponsor will select a portfolio of assets for their partnership that will be comparable in quality and results to the portfolios the sponsor has built for its successful partnerships in the past.

Some say the past is a prologue to the future, but it is not always an accurate tool for predicting future economic performance of general partners. To be sure, some general partners meet or exceed projected investment goals. Others, often with the best of intentions, are unable to do so because of changing market conditions or the unavailability of appropriate properties. A small number simply mismanage their partnerships. In any case, it is a foregone conclusion that a certain percentage of new issue partnerships will not meet their stated goals. The problem is knowing beforehand which ones these will be.

Such blind faith is not required to buy a partnership interest in the secondary market. The partnerships traded on the secondary market have survived their start-up phase, perhaps the riskiest time of any investment. They own all their assets and are well on their way to realizing—or failing to reach—their investment goals. If performance has proven lower than projected, this is reflected in lower prices offered for units, because all partnerships are competing on the same playing field. Buyers are paying for actual assets and demonstrated cash flow, not projections. An ample supply of units from solid performing partnerships means that ones with troubled asset portfolios tend not to trade at all.

The proven performance issue alone is an excellent reason why financial advisers and investors should investigate the partnership secondary market. But there are other advantages, as well.

Shorter Holding Periods

Partnerships traded in the secondary market offer quicker paybacks than new issues. Typically, buyers are not interested in partnerships that haven't existed for at least two years, and many units available on the market are from partnerships that are at least ten years old. Because they have already made substantial progress within the normal 10-year to 15-year investment cycle, the asset holding period of the secondary unit is compressed. Entering the investment midway through its life cycle means that the buyer can look forward to liquidation within a shorter time frame than the buyer of a new-issue partnership.

Potential Tax Benefits

Current tax law does not allow offsetting passive income (from partnerships) with ordinary or portfolio losses (from non-partnership investments). Consider an investor who has passive income from investments, such as maturing real estate limited partnerships in the asset sale phase, for example, that can't be offset because the investor doesn't own any investments generating passive losses. Passive income can be sheltered by purchasing proven passive loss generators in the secondary market, thereby neutralizing the overall tax burden of the investment portfolio.

Conversely, an investor's portfolio may be generating an excess amount of passive tax losses that are going to waste because of the absence of passive income, which can be offset with passive losses. For instance, an investor may have placed money in a number of deep tax shelters in the early eighties whose benefits have become practically unusable because of tax reform. One solution may be to purchase units in the secondary market that generate passive income; in that way, the passive losses can be used up. Another solution might be to use the secondary market to sell one of the partnership investments yielding passive losses, which could generate enough of a gain to eat up the excess losses still remaining in the portfolio.

Low Transaction Cost

The "front-end" costs of investing are significantly lower than those in primary partnership issues. In a secondary market purchase, the buyer has to pay only a brokerage commission for the trade (typically 5 percent to 8 percent of the transaction amount), which means that a greater percentage of the buyer's investment dollars is placed in the partnership's assets. In primary issues, fees of 15 percent to 25 percent come off the top of the investment right away to cover legal, accounting, organizational and marketing expenses, which means that of a $10,000 initial investment, as little as $7,500 may be end up being applied to asset acquisitions. On the secondary market, out of a $10,000 initial investment, fully $9,200 to $9,500 typically will be applied to acquiring assets. And, in some cases, the discount is large enough so that the $10,000 investment buys more than $10,000 in equity, even after commissions!

Immediate Investment Returns

Primary-issue partnerships typically go through a start-up phase, also called the funding period, during which capital is solicited from new investors. After a specified minimum amount of capital is raised (known as the impound amount), the funds are released from an escrow account and can be used for the acquisition of capital assets. Reaching the impound mark alone can take several months, and then the partnership may or may not have enough ready capital to begin building its portfolio. While the partnership continues to raise funds, the capital that has already been raised sits in a money market fund of the general partner's choosing, earning interest at going money market rates. Although the general partner may initiate quarterly distributions to limited partners at this time, these distributions don't reflect the partnership's investment performance. The payments most often represent a combination of money market interest and may even include a partial return of the investors' own contributed capital.

Sometimes, too, the influx of investor capital doesn't occur quickly enough to support a high enough volume of asset acquisitions. Consequently, the start-up phase can last as long as two years until the partnership gets fully funded, and sometimes even longer before all the assets are bought. For all intents and purposes during this time, the limited partner's investment (less the 15 percent to 25 percent taken out in fees) sits idly by.

Not so with an investment in the secondary market. Because the investor buys into an existing partnership with an already operational portfolio of assets, there is no waiting involved. The buyer knows that he or she can immediately begin to receive cash flow distributions—often within two months of the investment—and can see that these distributions result directly from asset operations.

Further, in cases in which the partnership has acquired all of its assets but hasn't yet begun to sell them, secondary market buyers may find themselves in a particularly advantageous position. Many prospectuses state that limited partners must get back their original investment, of, say, $1,000 per unit, plus a specified cumulative annual return, before the general partner begins sharing in partnership profits. When a secondary market buyer purchases an existing partnership, he or she is treated, for all practical purposes, just like the original unit owner. In other words, even if the buyer acquires the units at a 50 percent discount, for $500 per unit, the unit's original offering price ($1,000) will have to be returned to comply with the return requirements stated in the prospectus.

Excellent Values

When limited partners decide to sell their units, they are striving to transform a long-term, illiquid investment into a liquid asset. Would you give $100 in cash to someone who offered you a note for $100 that wouldn't be paid off for three or four years? Of course not, but you might consider giving him $25 or $50. The cash needs of sellers in the secondary market and the corresponding service offered by buyers translate into a simple fact: units are sold at a discount from their actual value. The market exists, and is growing, because it offers buyers the opportunity to acquire assets for a relatively low price. Investors can buy assets at a discount because they are in a position to give sellers cash today for an investment that may take several years to mature.

To accomplish their objective, sellers accept a price that discounts the unit's value. What sellers give up in value, buyers gain in value. The buyer obtains assets at a discounted price and within a compressed time frame, creating an attractive equity position. The fact that limited partnership units are thinly traded, like certain over-the-counter stocks, creates the opportunity for some very good investments, indeed. For the long-term investor, the secondary market for partnership interests can be an excellent arena in which to build a portfolio of assets with an outstanding ratio of fairly low risk and relatively high rewards.

HOW TO INVEST IN THE MARKET

Attractive as these advantages are, the secondary market isn't for everyone. The aftermarket for limited partnerships is a highly specialized one with its own set of requirements for buyers. Buyers in the market fall within one of two categories: those who buy pre-owned units for their own account, similar in some ways to picking individual corporate stocks, and those who place their money in privately offered pooled funds—similar to mutual funds—that build and manage portfolios of units on their behalf.

Individual Investing

The individual investors who purchase or trade public partnerships on their own must have either a $75,000 net worth or a combined $30,000 net worth and $30,000 annual income. They buy pre-owned units through brokers or financial planners, who often work with a (secondary market) dealer to effect unit trades. The entire process is quite similar to buying an over-the-counter stock. (See Figure 3.3.)

FIGURE 3.3 Parties to Secondary Market Transactions

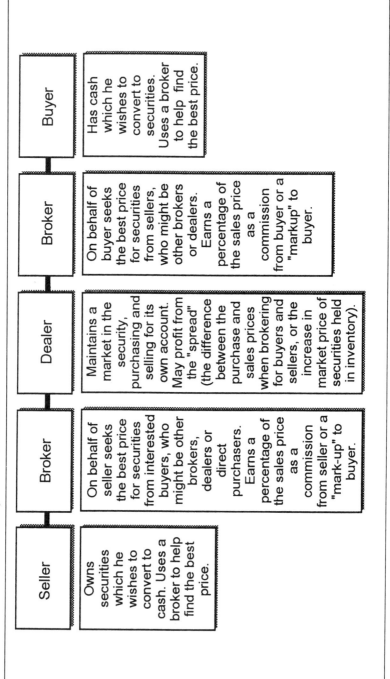

Seller

Owns securities which he wishes to convert to cash. Uses a broker to help find the best price.

Broker

On behalf of seller seeks the best price for securities from interested buyers, who might be other brokers, dealers or direct purchasers. Earns a percentage of the sales price as a commission from seller or a "mark-up" to buyer.

Dealer

Maintains a market in the security, purchasing and selling for its own account. May profit from the "spread" (the difference between the purchase and sales prices when brokering for buyers and sellers, or the increase in market price of securities held in inventory).

Broker

On behalf of buyer seeks the best price for securities from sellers, who might be other brokers or dealers. Earns a percentage of the sales price as a commission from buyer or a "markup" to buyer.

Buyer

Has cash which he wishes to convert to securities. Uses a broker to help find the best price.

While a few dealers will deal directly with investors, most work exclusively through brokers or financial planners. The larger ones may work with a network of thousands of brokers. When an investor calls directly and expresses an interest in buying or selling units, they will put the individual in touch with one or more brokers or financial planners, since their practice is to "wholesale" partnership units through their trading desk, rather than "retail" them directly to investors. However, when a broker or planner calls and expresses an interest in buying a quantity of a certain partnership, their traders will talk to the broker/planner—and sometimes to the client as well—to determine if indeed that particular purchase will best serve the client's needs. The dealer's trading experts may offer alternative suggestions based on the client's broad investment objectives and tolerance for risk, and in consideration of up-to-the-minute information on how the available partnerships are performing.

An example of special services dealers may offer to help securities representatives serve their clients is the special computer-generated "model portfolio." Say a broker calls because a client wants to invest $100,000 in a particular partnership. Discussion with the broker reveals that the client is primarily interested in income and safety, so the dealer assists the broker in putting together a model portfolio of income partnerships, which will diversify the investment and lower risk. This enables the broker and client to see at a glance how a particular investment mix will fare. As the sample income portfolio in Figure 3.4 shows, a $100,430 investment in four different partnerships, 65 percent in low-leverage real estate and 35 percent in equipment leasing, would provide the investor with an overall yield of 11.41 percent per annum. This specific partnership mix was created by a dealer firm based on an evaluation of the client's investment goals. Initially, the client may have asked his or her broker to purchase $100,000 of a particular income-oriented real estate partnership yielding 9 percent. After some discussion, the dealer's traders recognized that the client's objective was to obtain as high a rate of current income as possible. Accordingly, the sample income portfolio was generated to compare to the originally sought-after real estate partnership. The comparison clearly showed the difference in yield to the investor, and it

FIGURE 3.4 Income Portfolio

Portfolio Features	Asset Allocation
Yield: 11.48%	Real Estate: 65%
Leverage: None	Leasing: 35%

Park Properties V (PP 5)
Portfolio of four mobile home parks located in four states.

Insured Properties 1985 (IP 85)
Insured triple-net lease payments and underlying land leases on 242 restaurant properties in 35 states.

Aircraft Income Partners I (AIP 1)
Portfolio of McDonnell and Boeing aircraft leased to seven different airlines.

Growth Fund IV (GF 4)
Diversified portfolio of aircraft, marine vessels and railcars.

Partnership	Units	Price/ Unit	Amnt. Invested	Annual Distr./ Unit	Tot. Ann. Dist.	Yield on Client Cost	% of Portfolio
PP 5 - RE	250	$89	$22,250	$7.42	$1,855.00	8.34%	22%
IP 85 - RE	100	$430	$43,000	$45.03	$4,503.00	10.47%	43%
AIP 1 - LE	90	$260	$23,400	$42.50	$3,825.00	16.35%	23%
GF 4 - LE	620	$19	$11,780	$2.06	$1,277.20	10.84%	12%

Total Invested: $100,430   Total Distr.: $11,460.20   11.41%

became apparent that the recommended portfolio of partnerships would meet the client's income and safety goals better than the single partnership in which the client originally expressed an interest.

Similarly, a client may believe strongly in portfolio diversification by asset category and therefore want to spread his or her total investment dollars among four major asset categories—real estate, equipment leasing, oil and gas, and cable TV—placing 25 percent of available funds in each category. Assume this investor is young and wants to maximize equity growth, rather than

FIGURE 3.5   Growth Portfolio

Portfolio Features	Asset Allocation
Yield: 5.87%	Real Estate: 78%
Leverage: None	Cable: 22%

Income Properties XII (IP12)
Three office buildings and three retail properties. The properties are located in three different states (New York, California and Missouri)

Cable TV Investors V (CTV 5)
Portfolio of moderately leveraged television cable systems. Appraised value of $525 per $500 original unit.

Capital Income Properties VIII (CIP 8)
Four office and three retail properties. 32% of the portfolio long term net-leased. Average occupancy of more than 90%. Properties in four states.

Realty Investors IV (RI 4)
The partnership consists of six all-cash apartments in Florida, Arizona and Texas.

Partnership	Units	Price/ Unit	Amnt. Invested	Annual Dist./Unit	Tot. Ann. Dist.	Yield on Client Cost	% of Portfolio
IP 12 - RE	50	$550	$27,500	$40.00	$2,000.00	7.27%	28%
CTV 5 - CA	70	$315	$22,050	$0.00	$0.00	0.00%	22%
CIP 8 - RE	50	$540	$27,000	$35.00	$1,750.00	6.48%	27%
RI 4 - RE	100	$234	$23,400	$21.20	$2,120.00	9.06%	23%
		Total Invested:	$99,950		Total Distr.: $5,870.00	5.87%	

current income. The model growth portfolio in Figure 3.5 shows how omitting equipment leasing and energy partnerships (both with highly uncertain futures) and placing a heavier emphasis on real estate and cable TV would better suit the investor's overall investment objectives. By looking at an actual portfolio of existing partnerships, the client can make a better informed investment decision.

The individuals most successful in trading for their own account through brokers or planners typically spend some time getting to know the partnerships that are available for sale. Unlike the primary market for partnerships, the aftermarket doesn't offer glossy marketing brochures and slick sales kits. The investor's broker or planner may have to review the partnership's financial statements, read an independently prepared research report and talk at length with the market traders who are familiar with the security. But doing this type of homework can really pay off. The investors who have an idea of what they want and what's available are getting some of the best deals available in the market.

Pooled Investment Funds

A variety of secondary market pooled funds are available to investors. Similar in many ways to mutual funds, these private placement offerings (which are in themselves limited partnerships) give investors the opportunity to participate in a select, well-diversified portfolio of discounted partnerships, which may be comprised of real estate, cable TV and equipment leasing partnerships. In essence, they are a "fund of funds." The suitability requirements for participation often specify high income or high net worth—typically earnings of $200,000 for the past two years, with the expectation of earning the same amount in the current year, or, alternatively, a net worth of $1 million. These high suitability standards define an "accredited investor", that is, one who ostensibly possesses a high degree of investment sophistication and the wherewithal to make a substantial investment. Many of these partnerships are also open to nonaccredited investors.

Such pooled funds, available through two or three investment firms, typically require a minimum investment of $25,000 to $50,000. Each fund raises an average of $5 million from a total of 99 investors, then launches into acquiring a most highly diversified portfolio of a specific type of partnership, such as real estate assets. The fund acts as a secondary market buyer, purchasing units from 20 to 50 different limited partnerships, many of which have diverse management styles and investment strategies. This

FIGURE 3.6 Pooled Fund Structure

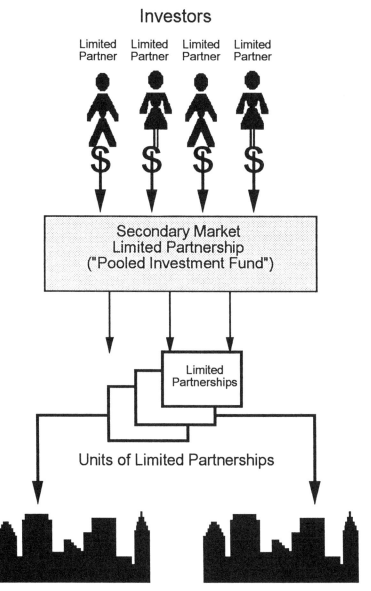

FIGURE 3.7   Example of Pooled Fund Portfolio Diversification
(Liquidity Fund Growth Plus Partners 1991)

Overall Diversification:

Number of different partnerships:....................................33
Number of different general partners:............................22
Total number of properties:...176

Property Diversification:

Property Type	Number	Percentage of Value
Apartment	73	41%
Retail	33	19%
Office	27	15%
Mobile home	3	1%
Other	42	24%

Geographic Diversification:

Region	Apts	Retail	Office	Mobile Home	Other	Total
California	8	4	3	3	3	21
Northwest	0	1	3	0	5	9
Mountain	3	0	0	0	0	3
Southwest	10	4	4	0	8	26
Southeast	32	18	7	0	18	75
Midwest	12	3	4	0	3	22
Northeast	8	3	6	0	5	22
Totals:	73	33	27	3	42	178

acquisition strategy automatically provides a second level of
diversification because, for example, each real estate partnership
acquired by the fund typically owns from 1 to 20 different
properties. This means that such a fund offers substantial asset
diversification, acquiring mature limited partnership interests in
as many as several hundred different properties! (See Figures
3.6 and 3.7.)

The funds purchase units at an average discount of 40 percent
to 50 percent from "break-up" value. Break-up value is deter-

mined independently of a partnership's general partners and represents an estimate of what the units would actually be worth if the partnership were immediately liquidated; that is, if all the assets were sold today, all liabilities paid off and the proceeds distributed at once according to the priority return requirements set out in the partnership prospectus. The break-up value is determined by in-depth research that considers such factors as (1) the performance of the partnership to date based on scrutiny of the financial statements, (2) the current stage of the partnership's life cycle, (3) a detailed property-by-property analysis of the assets, including an analysis of current market conditions where each property is located and projections for future occupancy and rents, and (4) an evaluation of the terms of the prospectus specifying priority returns and profit sharing between general and limited partners.

Independent estimates of break-up value by dealers or analysts for these funds sometimes range from 10 percent to 20 percent below the general partners' own estimates of liquidation, or net asset, value. Why would this discrepancy exist? In general, independent analysts tend to be less optimistic about local real estate market conditions and the salability of a particular property, conservatively assuming it would sell near the middle range of recent comparable sales, while the general partners, just like homeowners who put the family house on the market, tend to attach a higher value to their properties.

The funds' analysts derive the discount from break-up value they require to purchase by using a computer model. The model determines the price that should be paid in order to obtain a desired return on investment. Return on investment estimates are based on:

1. An assumption that the partnership will sell its remaining assets over a specified period of time (usually seven to ten years, depending on the partnership); and
2. An assumption that the assets will experience a growth rate of a specified percentage per year (determined by an appraisal of the markets in which the properties are located).

The funds stand as a ready buyer, with cash in hand, for units of a carefully selected group of target partnerships, some of which are lesser known, thinly traded ones. Their bid prices are based on the funds' detailed analyses of the investment return the units will yield and the relative safety of the investment, measured by the funds' confidence in the general partners' ability to perform.

The funds perform an extremely thorough due diligence review of the partnerships, and the units are bought at a deep enough discount to generate a highly competitive return to the investors relative to the risk of the investment. With the lesser known partnerships, rather than prices being established by external market forces of supply and demand—as they tend to be for the better known, more closely followed and frequently traded partnerships—the funds often are able to set their own prices for the partnerships they acquire, based on their investment needs and objectives.

The funds themselves collect front-end fees that reflect the costs of organization, raising capital, researching potential partnership acquisitions and advertising to prospective sellers. These front-end fees, like those in a primary issue partnership, average about 25 percent of contributed capital. Therefore, of one dollar placed in a fund, about 75 cents may be available for investment in partnership units. But because the partnerships are bought at such deep discounts, 40 percent to 50 percent below current break-up value, the actual value of one dollar invested, in terms of the underlying equity it purchases, even after the organizational fee is deducted, is immediately boosted to $1.10 to $1.20. (See Figure 3.8.)

Pros and Cons of Pooled Fund Investing

For a wealthy investor who can afford the initial investment, these pooled funds provide several significant advantages. Most notable is the benefit of participating in an exclusive, privately managed investment orchestrated by a professional investment manager. Investing in a fund provides the means to letting a research firm select and manage a portfolio of partnerships that it believes will perform extremely well on the investor's behalf.

Extensive diversification is another important benefit; the 20 to 50 partnerships acquired in each fund vary in management

FIGURE 3.8   How $1 Can Buy $1.11 of Assets in a Secondary Market
Pooled Fund

Amount Invested:	$1.00
Fund Organization Costs:	(.25)
Cash for Buying Assets:	.75
Discount from Break-up Value of Assets Acquired:	40%
Percentage of Asset Value Paid for Assets:	60%
Assets Bought Per Dollar Paid:	$.75 divided by .60 or $1.25
General Partner Share:	11% or (.14)
Limited Partner Share:	89% or $1.11

style, property type and property location. Such high diversification significantly reduces risk and increases the probability of attaining projected performance goals.

Additionally, the funds often incorporate careful tax planning strategies into their acquisition plans. For example, some of the partnerships that are acquired may generate taxable losses; these can then be balanced by partnerships that provide taxable income. The well-thought-out blending of tax offsetting partnerships can thus create a tax-neutral effect, resulting in partially to fully tax-sheltered positive cash flow.

A disadvantage to investing in a pooled fund, as opposed to individually buying units, is the larger investment size and higher suitability requirement; not everyone has the means or even the desire to plunk down $25,000 to $50,000 for an investment in the secondary market. An investor can, alternatively, make a much smaller investment by researching partnerships and building a portfolio of units on his or her own.

Of course, some individuals prefer to control their own investments—to handpick them on their own. They do so with stocks, bonds, artwork and all their other investments, and tend as a rule to shy away from mutual funds and other professionally managed vehicles. Often it is simply a question of investment style.

Another disadvantage to pooled fund investing concerns possible delays in income tax filing. Because the fund itself is a limited partner in 20 to 50 limited partnerships, the investor in the fund essentially becomes a limited partner of a limited partner. In its own capacity as a limited partner, the fund receives K-1 tax filing information from all the partnerships in which it holds interests and must then, in turn, condense the information into one, cohesive K-1 statement for its own investors that reflects the investors' pro rata share of the fund's net income. Limited partnerships are notoriously slow in producing and delivering K-1s to their partners. Thus, K-1 statements trickle into the fund over a period of time, and before the fund can sort, analyze and present the information in K-1s to its investors, the April 15 tax filing deadline may have already passed.

Fund investors often find themselves having to extend their tax return filing date, an increasingly common phenomenon that is now automatically accepted by the IRS. In recognition of this problem, some funds provide their investors with estimates in November of expected income for the year. For income tax filing, the investors then have two options: They can file their tax returns by April 15, using the early estimates provided by the fund, and file an amended return in August; or they can pay an estimated tax and extend, filing their tax return after April 15. (See Figure 3.9.)

BUYER SUITABILITY

Transfers of limited partnership units on the partnership's books depend on the incoming partner's meeting the same

FIGURE 3.9   An Individual Purchase of Partnerships Compared to a
Pooled Fund Purchase of Partnerships in the Limited
Partnership Secondary Market

	Individual Purchase	Pooled Fund Purchase
Selection of Partnerships:	By individual	By professional researchers
Management:	By individual	By professional managers
Diversification:	1 — 5 partnerships	20 — 50 partnerships
Taxation:	Can vary substantially with each partnership resulting in excess passive income or excess passive gains	Diversification permits blending for tax-neutral effect
Number of annual partnership tax reports (K-1s):	1 — 5	1
Delivery date of K-1s:	Varies with each partnership	Tax estimate delivered early for timely income tax filing. Final K-1 delivered after last partnership reports to fund managers
Minimum Investment:	$5,000 — $20,000	$25,000 — $50,000

minimum suitability standards as the original owner. These
suitability standards vary from partnership to partnership, but
all revolve around income and net worth requirements. Even
within a particular partnership, the standards can vary from
state to state (depending on where the limited partner resides),
but the prospectus clearly spells out any such variances. The

suitability standards for investment in a pooled fund (i.e., the necessity of being an accredited investor) are high enough so that the fund investors are certain to be suitable for all of the partnerships acquired.

Individual buyers, however, must make sure that they conform to the specific original suitability standards of the partnership(s) they wish to purchase. Each partnership has different requirements for proof of suitability. Some insist on receiving documentation attesting to the incoming partner's suitability; others require no proof at all. In purchasing units through a broker or dealer, the buyer will often receive copies of those pages in the prospectus describing the investor suitability requirements, along with a statement to sign that proclaims his or her conformity to them.

HOW TO COPE WITH THE SPECTER OF PHANTOM GAIN

"Phantom Gain" is a tax liability that can occur when a secondary market buyer's basis (purchase price) of a limited partnership unit is much higher than the original limited partner's basis (property's book value). When the property sells, the new limited partner must pay taxes on the gain (sale price less the *original* limited partner's basis). The difference between the original partner's basis and the new partner's basis represents a gain on the sale from which the new limited partner never realizes corresponding monetary benefit.

For example, assume that the selling partner originally paid $1,000 for each limited partnership unit, and has received cumulative tax write-offs totaling $1,000, so that the original limited partner's tax basis is zero at the time of a secondary market sale. Now suppose that the unit had a net asset value of $500, based on two assets of equal value remaining in the partnership's portfolio. The secondary market buyer decides that a 20 percent discount sounds reasonable, so he bids $400 per unit. If the partnership were to liquidate one of its remaining two assets the next day, the new limited partner would yield a real gain (in cash) of $50 on his proportional interest. Phantom gain from the sale,

FIGURE 3.10 The Effect of a "754 Election"

	Without the Section 754 Election	With the Section 754 Election
Value of unit	$500	$500
Sales price for one of the two remaining assets	$250	$250
50 percent of $400/unit purchase price (representing a 20 percent discount from net asset value)	(200)	(200)
Cash gain on sale	$ 50	$ 50
Tax	(100)*	(20)**
Net after-tax gain (loss)	$(50)	$ 30

*Without the Section 754 election, the tax incurred is 40 percent of the $250 sales price since the tax basis is zero. A deduction for this "extra" tax paid can be taken at the time of the partnership's dissolution, but, because one asset still remains in the portfolio, this event may be years away and of little present value.

**With the Section 754 election, the tax incurred is 40 percent of the actual gain on sale.

however, based on the unit's zero tax basis, would amount to an additional $200 (based on the difference between the sale price and the zero basis), on which the investor would also have to pay taxes. In partnerships where the unit's tax basis drops below zero, new partners can be faced with even greater phantom gain tax liabilities.

General partners can make an accounting adjustment on the partnership's books (called a Section 754 election) that enables a unit buyer to avoid assuming the lower tax basis of the selling partner. This adjustment is not simple, however, since it entails frequently adjusting the tax basis of the individual assets of a partnership, and maintaining separate books for each limited partner. The partnership's prospectus usually states whether the general partner has elected to do this or not.

The Section 754 adjustment effectively protects the secondary buyer from incurring phantom gain tax liabilities. It thus enables original limited partners to realize more value for their interests when they sell them into the secondary market, since the prospect of phantom gains induces buyers to significantly cut their bid prices to offset the expected tax liability.

If our buyer in the above example were in a 40 percent tax bracket (combined federal and state), the tax effects of his purchase can be compared as in Figure 3.10.

Highly leveraged partnerships that provided their partners with substantial tax write-offs in their early years are most likely to generate phantom gains. Buyers need to recognize the likelihood of phantom gain in these cases. While the general partner will not make a Section 754 election (in most cases), the price bid for the units should be discounted enough to compensate for the potential tax liability.

Fund investment managers cautiously consider the prospect of phantom gain as they pursue their partnership acquisition strategies. This is one factor that can drive them to purchase units at deep discounts from the partnerships' net asset values and from their own estimates of break-up values.

HOW TO BUY SMART IN THE SECONDARY MARKET

The best strategies for buying in the secondary market depend on the individual investor's financial capabilities and needs. For an accredited investor who has an interest in real estate (or, in one or two cases, equipment leasing partnerships), private pooled funds provide the greatest asset diversification. Under the aegis of an experienced investment manager, the fund participant can sit back and enjoy the benefits of a professionally researched, well-selected and professionally administered portfolio of diverse partnership units. The investor's only obligation is making the initial investment, receiving periodic distribution checks and filing the required tax reporting information. Everything else is handled on the investor's behalf.

For an individual who doesn't meet the high suitability requirements imposed by the private placement fund offerings, or who prefers to select and follow secondary market investments on his or her own, a number of options exist. Individual buyers can create and manage "minifunds" of their own, choosing a portfolio of limited partnership units that will perform to achieve a specific set of investment objectives. Alternatively, the buyer may want to invest in only one partnership or in only one asset category. In any case, it is essential to work with a broker or planner who is able to gather and analyze information about specific partnerships so that the investor can truly do some "comparison shopping." Brokers and planners, in turn, should develop relationships with one or more of the established dealers so they can take advantage of their research, analysis and computerized models.

So many variables affect estimated break-up value, potential tax consequences and projected income or growth that "gut" decisions simply don't make sense in this market. Opportunities for profits in the secondary market may abound, but the truly smart way to invest is with a clear definition of investment objectives, close scrutiny of alternative investments and carefully orchestrated diversification.

CHAPTER 4

Valuation Techniques and Investment Strategies

Investing in the partnership secondary market may sound like a winning proposition, and it can be, but only if the investment is valued and priced appropriately. The most important function performed by potential buyers in the market, as in any securities market, involves analyzing the securities in enough depth to ascertain (1) the strength of the assets backing them and (2) what price to pay for them to help shape the investor's desired return. The determination of price in relation to the investment's current and future potential will, to a great extent, dictate whether, and the extent to which, the buyer ultimately profits from the purchase.

PARTNERSHIP VALUE ANALYSIS

Evaluating pre-owned partnership units and identifying ones that are investment-worthy requires several methodical steps and much diligence. It is not unusual for a careful market-making firm, for example, to look at as many as 100 to 200 different partnerships to find only one or two that it considers worth buying.

Real estate partnerships are analyzed differently from partnerships in cable TV, equipment leasing, or oil and gas. Nonetheless, the first steps are similar. The first question is the goal of the buyer. If an individual or dealer is buying for resale purposes, to whom will the resale be made? What type of partnerships are potential purchasers looking for? If the purchase is to be made for a long-term hold, then what specific investment criteria are to be used? Answering these questions will set general guidelines for the type of partnership to look at. One can then go through SEC filings and trade publications to identify partnerships that are candidates for evaluation.

The next question is whether there is adequate seller interest. Have dealers had requests from sellers for evaluations? Is the partnership large enough to be worth evaluating? Have any trades occurred in the partnership? Once a partnership passes these first screens—that it meets the criteria of interested buyers or investors, and that there is adequate seller interest to be worth evaluating—the next step is a rough review of the partnership's current operational status. This is accomplished by obtaining as much information about the partnership as possible. Initially, the dealer will avail itself of industry publications, such as Stanger's *Investment Advisor, The Wall Street Journal*, Partnership Profiles' *The Perspective*, and information published by Standard & Poor's to find out what types of assets are owned, where the assets are located and to get a picture of the partnership in relation to other partnerships in the same asset class.

If it appears that the partnership has value, the individual investor, broker or dealer's securities analyst may then seek to obtain more in-depth information to begin assembling a rough analysis. This might include the original offering prospectus, original registration statements and other documents filed by the general partners with the SEC, and forms 10K, 10Q and 8K. (For a modest fee, the Washington, D.C.-based firm Disclosure, Inc., provides copies of these forms and all other public information filed with the SEC.)

DETERMINING VALUE IN A
REAL ESTATE PARTNERSHIP

From this point, analytical techniques vary greatly with different types of partnerships. Determining the break-up value of a real estate partnership provides a good example of the depth of research and analysis that is essential to prudent investing in the secondary market, but the analysis of other types of partnerships will be different. For real estate partnerships, the analyst's first goal is to evaluate a partnership's exact current net asset position—the total value of all partnership assets, less all partnership liabilities. From that figure the break-up value can be determined—what limited partners would get, today, if the partnership immediately liquidated all of its assets, paid off its liabilities and distributed all the proceeds in accordance with the priorities set forth in the partnership agreement. A partnership's break-up value can be estimated only if you first estimate what the partnership's assets are worth, plus how much cash the partnership has in reserves.

How do you estimate the worth of a partnership asset? It is worth exactly what it can be sold for at current market prices. Occasionally, an analyst will assign zero equity to troubled properties (e.g., a leveraged office building with high vacancy rates and little operating income) or other assets in a partnership's portfolio. If such an asset is subsequently given up through foreclosure, nothing is lost since the unit buyer didn't pay anything for it (unless the property, in addition, carries tax liabilities with it). Conversely, if such a "zero value" property is eventually turned around and sold, the buyer will get an extra return on the investment that was not counted on in the partnership analysis and evaluation.

In estimating current market values, the analyst may use a capitalization (cap) rate on the properties' net operating income. Cap rates vary from one area of the country to another and from one type of property to another. Based on sales of comparable properties within the last 90 days, for example, cap rates may be higher overall in Dallas than they are in Seattle, so applying local market cap rates allows a realistic determination of how much properties could sell for in the local market, and whether the assets have enough value to cover the partnership's debt. (See Figure 4.1.)

Analysts often use market contacts across the country to help evaluate a partnership's properties. Some dealers have many contacts, which include real estate agents, brokers, appraisers

FIGURE 4.1   Using the Cap Rate To Determine Real Estate Value

The capitalization (cap) rate is a method of determining property value based on an evaluation of the property's net operating income. Net operating income is the property's rental and other income, less operating expenses, maintenance, insurance and taxes. Mortgage payments are excluded, so the calculation determines exactly how much a property would earn if owned without any financing.

If a particular office building, for example, is generating $50,000 in net operating income per year, and a buyer pays $500,000 for the building, the cap rate is 10% (net operating income divided into the purchase price). In many market areas, cap rates of 9% to 11% are the norm. An analyst can look at net operating income, divide by the local cap rate and roughly determine the building's current market value, i.e., what price the building would fetch if it were sold today. For example, if the partnership being analyzed owned a multifamily garden apartment complex generating net operating income of $100,000 per year, the analyst could use a 10 percent cap rate to determine that the building was currently worth approximately $1 million. The estimated market value is then fine-tuned by taking into consideration deferred maintenance, average vacancy rates, location and other factors that will affect how much a buyer is willing to pay.

and property managers. In addition to information gleaned from the partnership's financial statements and other written documentation, an analyst will often rely on the opinion of these local real estate professionals to help determine property values in a local market. The goal is to use every means possible to piece together an accurate and realistic market value of all the assets.

If a dealer acquires, on the behalf of clients, a substantial position in a given partnership ($500,000 or more), it may choose to augment its analytical approach by sending its own real estate professionals out to the properties to directly appraise values by examining the structures, evaluating the state of property maintenance and talking with the property managers.

PRIORITY RETURNS AND
SHARING ARRANGEMENTS

After the current net asset value of a partnership is estimated, the analyst must ascertain whether any person or entity has a priority claim on the partnership's cash flow or assets. For example, if a partnership experienced a net operating loss, the general partners may have felt that the situation would have improved in time. Consequently, they themselves may have made a loan or a number of loans to the partnership to help keep it afloat long enough for economic recovery to occur. This, in fact, was a common practice during the late eighties among some of the stronger general partners and sponsors in real estate, who considered it to be in the best interests of the limited partners to hold the assets and wait until market conditions improved, rather than liquidate the portfolio and take a loss.

The analyst also must look at any profit-sharing or joint-venture arrangements that affect asset ownership, because a partnership's assets may not be owned 100 percent by the partnership. For instance, in construction/development projects, joint ventures between a partnership and a real estate developer are common. In such a case, the partnership contracts with the developer to build an office building, shopping center or multifamily residential complex, typically supplying construction financing and/or purchasing the land on which the building or buildings are to be built. The developer bears planning, architectural and construction management costs. A joint-venture agreement between the developer and the partnership specifies a certain sharing arrangement for the building's ongoing cash flow (from rental income) and for the proceeds from the eventual sale. If the developer doesn't put up-front cash into the project, the partnership usually receives a priority return from cash flow up to a designated amount; then cash flow is split in a specified ratio between the partnership and developer. Sales proceeds in excess of property liabilities are shared in the same way. (See Figure 4.2.)

Finally, partnership analysts scrutinize the partnership's limited partnership agreement and all of its relevant amendments and supplements concerning profit-sharing arrangements

FIGURE 4.2 Joint-Venture Arrangements

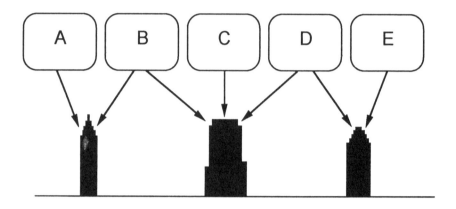

A) Partnerships Share Ownership to
Diversify Portfolio and Spread Risk

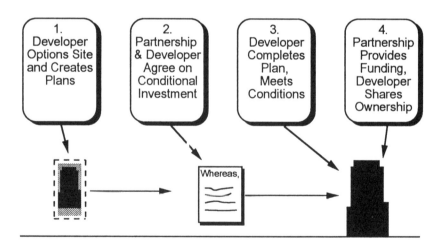

B) Developer and Partnership Develop a Property

between the limited and general partners to find out where the partnership is in its investment cycle and how much of an investment return limited partners can still obtain. The partnership agreement is contained within the original registration statement (prospectus), often under the heading of "Allocation of Net Profits, Net Losses, Distributable Cash from Operations and Surplus Funds." A close look at these sharing arrangements is critical. Although a limited partnership unit might seem to be a good buy based on the profit-sharing arrangements between limited and general partners, all may not be as it first appears.

Limited partners typically receive a priority return from cash flow and have a cumulative return requirement that specifies that they receive a certain amount of cash back before the general partners can share in the partnership's net income from operations or profits from asset sales. The priority return and cumulative return requirements vary from partnership to partnership.

Here's a simplified example. The limited partners have a priority return equivalent to 6 percent per year on their original investment. After that priority return is met, funds are distributed 85 percent to the limited partners and 15 percent to the general partners. As assets are sold and capital is returned, limited partners must recoup 100 percent of their original investment first; then capital gains in excess of that amount are distributed 85 percent to limited partners and 15 percent to the general partner. Over eight years, the distribution of funds per $1,000 unit might look like this:

Year	Cap. Accnt.	Cash Flow Distr.	Ret. of Capital	Sub. Reserve
1	1,000	60	0	0
2	1,000	50	0	10
3	1,000	50	0	20
4	1,000	50	0	30
5	1,000	50	600	40
6	400	24	0	40
7	400	20	0	44
8	400	20	800*	48

*Part of this amount will be divided between limited and general partners since, together with prior capital returned of $600, it exceeds the sum of $1,000 per unit invested plus the remaining subordinated account.

In this example, the investor purchases units at $1,000, and has a priority return on cash flow from operations of 6 percent, or $60 per unit per year. The first year, $60 is paid out, so the 6 percent requirement is met, and nothing is entered into the subordinated reserve distribution. In year two, only $50 is paid out, so $10 is entered into the subordinated reserve distribution. Each year the partnership pays out less than 6 percent, the difference between the amount paid out and the priority return amount is added to the subordinated reserve amount.

In year five, $50 is paid out of cash flow from operations, so another $10 is added to the subordinated reserve distribution. But in addition, one of the partnership's properties is sold, netting $600 per unit as a return of capital. Since this $600 is a return of capital, and is not cash flow from operations, it has no effect on the amount still due limited partners in the subordinated reserve. However, when this $600 is paid to the limited partners, it reduces the capital account per unit to $400. Therefore, the 6 percent priority return in year six is based on a $400 capital account and is reduced to $24. In years seven and eight the subordinated reserve account increases by $4 per year and eventually totals $48. Also in year eight, the second property is sold, netting $800 per unit.

How will this $800 be distributed? First, the limited partners must receive their original investment back. Since $600 of capital was returned with the sale of the first property, the remaining $400 must be paid to limited partners from the proceeds of this sale. Further, the subordinated reserve amount of $48 must be paid to the limited partners to make up for the accumulated shortfalls from their 6 percent priority return. Thus, the first $448 dollars from the net proceeds of this sale go directly to the limited partners, leaving $352 per unit for distribution according to the 85/15 sharing arrangement between the limited and general partners. Eighty-five percent, or $299.20, goes to the limited partners and 15 percent, or $52.80, goes to the general partners.

Combine this variable in return percentages with joint-venture arrangements with developers that may also vary from property to property, and you have a complex revenue sharing situation, indeed.

"BREAK-UP" VALUE VS. "BOOK" VALUE:
WHAT ARE UNITS REALLY WORTH?

Many buyers express an interest in the units' original offering price and their current book value. For purposes of secondary market trading, however, neither of these numbers is truly significant. For a new investor about to assume ownership of existing units, all that really matters is the amount of value left in the units and the price at which the investor can acquire that value. Whether or not the units were originally sold as a new issue at an offering price of $1,000 per unit has no direct relationship to break-up value. If the current break-up value is $500 per unit, buyers will want to purchase that $500 value for less than $500, net of commissions.

It is worth pointing out that in most cases, the original $1,000 unit was never actually "worth" $1,000 anyway; the front-end sales commissions, also called the sales "load," typically removed anywhere from 15 percent to 25 percent of the invested capital right off the top, so of a $1,000 unit, perhaps only $750 was invested in assets. Therefore, looking at original offering price can be misleading.

The balance sheet calculation of book value also presents a distorted picture of what the units may actually be worth. Book value reflects only the original purchase price of the asset, less any mortgages or debt owed on the asset and depreciation, and computed according to precise accounting standards, called "generally accepted accounting principles," or GAAP. If any appreciation in asset value has occurred—as can be determined by applying cap rates to an increase in net income at an office building or multifamily complex that has increased its rents or decreased its vacancy rates—book value simply doesn't reflect it. Similarly, if the building has decreased in value through poor management or adverse local market conditions, book value won't reveal even a substantial loss in real (i.e., sellable) value. Finally, even if the asset's value hasn't changed, the continued annual automatic accounting deduction for depreciation will cause the book value to decline below the market value.

Clearly, then, determining the real current net asset value of each property in the partnership (as opposed to book value), the exact sharing arrangements and where the partnership is in its life cycle—i.e., how much has already been returned to limited partners in distributions, the level of the partnership's current cash flow and how many assets remain to be sold—is essential to establishing the break-up value per unit.

The analyst looks at all of these factors and, taking them into careful consideration, arrives at the per-unit break-up value— the estimated value that each unit would be worth to a current limited partner, in cash, if all the partnership's assets were immediately sold, the debts paid off and sales proceeds and cash distributed to limited and general partners according to current revenue sharing priorities. It is easy to understand why the review process typically takes from one to three weeks, depending on the degree of information the analyst already has on the partnership, before a dealer can decide if it will make an offer to buy units of a partnership it has not previously analyzed or acquired. (See Figures 4.3 and 4.4.)

JOINT VENTURES AND PROFIT SHARING

The most common type of joint venture that a partnership enters into is the joint purchase of assets by two or more limited partnerships, often "sister" partnerships sponsored by the same or related general partners. An example is the 1987 joint purchase of nine commercial properties by three Dean Witter partnerships, Dean Witter Realty Income Partnership III (Income III), Dean Witter Realty Income Partnership IV (Income IV), and Duportail Investment Partners (DPLP). The cash contributions from the three partnerships totaled $121,341,000, allocated as shown below:

Partnership	Capital Contribution	Percent
Income IV	$ 50,000,000	41.2%
Income III	32,430,000	26.7
DPLP	38,911,000	32.1
	$121,341,000	100.0%

FIGURE 4.3   Real Estate Limited Partnership Secondary Market
Evaluation Flow Chart

Locate

■ Identify target partnership from existing materials
    -SEC filings
    -Trade publications

■ Review financial statements and offering documents
    -Original offering prospectus
    -10K s, 10Q s and 8K s

Evaluate

■ Make in-depth analysis of financial statements
    -Partnership cash flow
    -Financial strength of partnership
    -Ratio analysis: current ratio, distribution coverage

■ Estimate current liquidation value
    -Assume all real estate sells today
    -Calculate distribution of all funds as required by
     offering documents and sharing arrangements

Determine Price

■ Determine appropriate discount
     - Run partnership simulation model
     - Make additional risk factor adjustments

FIGURE 4.4   Evaluating Equipment Leasing, Oil and Gas, and
Cable TV Partnerships

Equipment Leasing

Analyzing an equipment leasing partnership is significantly different from analyzing real estate units. A wide range of economic variables influence the profitability of an equipment leasing venture and the determination of the equipment's "residual value." Only if residual value is significant will the equipment partnership likely produce significant sales proceeds on top of its income stream, which ends at the end of the lease. For instance, fluctuations in world trade can have an adverse impact on marine container leasing; as the volume of world trade decreases, container leasing shows a corresponding decrease. Second, a weakening dollar would cause new containers, typically manufactured in the Far East, to escalate in price (although in this case, residual values would also increase for equipment taken out of leasing service). Similarly, for a partnership that leased airplanes, residual values plummet when airlines go out of business.

Technological developments can also affect values. If, for example, a new refrigerated container were developed that extended the transport life of produce, the existing containers would soon become obsolete. Leased computer equipment is often assumed to have no residual value because of the near certainty that it will be technologically outdated by the termination of the lease.

Evaluating these partnerships thus entails the analyst's ability to look into the future to try to forecast worldwide economic events as they affect conditions of supply and demand, and to anticipate advances in technology. Therefore, dealers tend to emphasize a partnership's most quantifiable results in determining unit value: i.e., current yield. Analysts may estimate some residual values based on the results of other partnerships in the same equipment industry, but because residual values depend to such a great extent on future unknowns, analysts give much more weight to current yield in determining the value of partnership units.

Oil and Gas

Other factors come into play with oil and gas partnerships. Oil wells are depleting assets, so in theory, each barrel pumped reduces the residual value of a well, assuming no changes in oil prices. Assets in an oil and gas partnership must be evaluated by looking at proven reserves, estimated reserves, the rate at which reserves are being pumped and current and projected market prices for oil and gas.

FIGURE 4.4   Evaluating Equipment Leasing, Oil and Gas, and
Cable TV Partnerships (continued)

Cable TV

Cable TV partnerships are valued according to current cash flow per subscriber, the size of the subscriber base and the potential for new subscribers and price increases. Thus a cable franchise that had achieved 50 percent penetration of a given market might be valued at less per subscriber than a franchise that had achieved only 25 percent penetration of a similar market area. Similarly, a franchise in a fast-growth suburban area might be valued at more per current subscriber than one in a no-growth urban area.

Of course, those percentage allocations between the partnerships apply only to the ownership of the specific asset they jointly purchased. Approximately seven months later, another joint venture was created between a different mix of affiliated partnerships. Dean Witter Realty Income IV purchased a 40.6 percent interest in an asset that had earlier been purchased jointly by Dean Witter Realty Income Partnership II and Dean Witter Realty Income Partnership III. Their respective capital contributions and percentages of ownership in this transaction after the Income IV investment were as follows:

Partnership	Capital Contribution	Percent
Income IV	$21,001,687	40.6%
Income II	7,687,500	14.8
Income III	23,062,500	44.6
	$51,751,687	100.0%

Thus, simple joint-venture arrangements become increasingly complex for the analyst to unravel when a partnership enters into several different ventures. Each property can be owned in different percentage amounts by a different mix of joint-venturing partnerships.

Another common joint-venture arrangement is between a partnership and a developer. In one typical agreement the proceeds from a sale or refinancing of the joint-venture properties were distributed according to the following priority arrangement:

- First, to the partnership, an amount equal to a 10 percent cumulative annual return on its capital contribution, as adjusted, reduced by certain prior distributions of net cash from operations to the partnership and any prior distributions of net proceeds from a sale or refinancing;
- Second, to the partnership, the next net proceeds up to an amount equal to 110 percent of its capital contribution;
- Third, 75 percent to the partnership and 25 percent to the developer until the partnership has received an amount equal to 110 percent of its capital contribution; and
- Fourth, the balance of any net proceeds, 50 percent to the partnership and 50 percent to the developer.

Assume the partnership's original capital contribution was $10 million and the net proceeds from the sale of the properties at the end of eight years was $24 million to be paid in two equal $12 million installments. If the partnership had received no prior distributions, then the first $8 million of the first installment would go to the partnership to meet the first priority, an amount equal to a 10 percent cumulative annual return on its original capital investment. The remaining $4 million from the first installment would repay a portion of the amount owed according to the second priority (110 percent of the original $10 million capital contribution), reducing the $11 million owed to the partnership to $7 million. When the next installment of $12 million arrived, $7 million of it would pay off the remaining amount due on the second priority, and the other $5 million would be divided 75 percent to the partnership and 25 percent to the developer in fulfillment of the third priority. According to this formula, the partnership would receive a 75 percent share of the second installment amounting to $9 million and 25 percent ($3 million) to the developer. (Any subsequent gains also would be divided at this 75 percent/25 percent rate until a total of $11 million was paid to the partnership in fulfillment of the third priority, after which all proceeds would be divided 50/50 in accordance with the fourth priority).

The outcome of each separate joint-venture arrangement depends upon each property's individual performance, and mistakes in appraising the current health and future outlook of a property can easily be magnified in cases such as these. For instance, consider a joint-venture arrangement in which the developer puts up cash and the partnership guarantees loans. The terms might specify that, after repayment of loans and accrued interest, the developer gets the first $1 million from sale, after which proceeds are split 75 percent to the partnership and 25 percent to the developer. Say the analyst estimates the property will sell for $10 million and net $2 million after payment of all loans and liabilities. In this case, $1.25 million of the net $2 million would go to the developer, and $750,000 to the partnership.

What if the analyst's estimate is 5 percent off and the building sells for only $9.5 million? The sale yields only $1.5 million for distribution after payment of all loans and liabilities. The developer gets the first $1 million plus 25 percent of the rest, for a total of $1.125 million. The partnership gets only $375,000. Because of the joint-venture sharing agreement, 5 percent error in estimating the value of a property is magnified into a 50 percent reduction in the actual income to the partnership!

SENSITIVITY ANALYSIS

Precisely because of the potential for error magnification, cautious analysts and dealers apply a "sensitivity" analysis to partnerships with any complexity of sharing arrangements. The analysts establish a hypothetical model on a computer spreadsheet enabling them to evaluate risks associated with different degrees of variation from estimates. In essence, a sensitivity analysis adds or subtracts a certain amount to the estimated value of each property (often between 1 percent and 3 percent) to see what effect the uncertainty factor will have on per-unit values. For example, say an analyst pegs the break-up value of a partnership at $650 per unit. A sensitivity analysis will look at several "what ifs." If you add 3 percent to the estimated salable value of all the properties in a portfolio, it may show that the terms of the joint-venture arrangements would have the overall effect of causing per-unit value to increase only $10 per unit because the bulk of the upside gain would go to the joint-venture partners. However, if you subtract 3 percent from the estimated sales prices, the per-unit value might fall to $500. In such a case, the sensitivity analysis would show that the purchase of these particular units is risky; if the portfolio performs 3 percent better than estimated, you stand to gain only $10 per unit, but if it performs 3 percent worse, you lose $150. Such a partnership may still be attractive as an investment, but the sensitivity analysis signals that you need to apply a greater discount to the purchase to balance the greater risk involved.

Of course, the sensitivity analysis can yield the opposite result as well. A partnership could offer far greater upside potential than downside risk. Each partnership is different in this regard. Some joint-venture sharing arrangements tend to magnify risk, while others lessen risk through diversification. For an unleveraged partnership that hasn't engaged in any joint ventures, a 3 percent change in value represents just that—3 percent. (See Figure 4.5.)

DATA MANAGEMENT

The more dedicated analysts and dealers maintain extensive working files on the public partnerships in which they have an interest. In some cases, as many as 1,500 different partnerships (of the more than 5,000 public partnerships created) may be on file, of which 300 to 400 are reviewed on a regular basis to continually update information. Maintaining accurate, up-to-date data on such a large number of partnerships is a complex process. Ongoing reviews include quarterly analyses of 10Qs, the quarterly financial statements filed with the Securities and Exchange Commission (SEC), a quarterly review of real estate values to make sure that occupancy rates and cash flow have not changed dramatically, and an in-depth annual property review to redetermine value in accordance with local real estate market trends.

FIGURE 4.5   Typical Partnership Pricing Analysis Chart

	Realty Growth Partnership
Year Formed:	1983
Initial Capitalization:	$30 million
Properties:	-Seven apartment complexes located in Southern California and Nevada -Three office buildings in New York City and Boston
Distributions:	$40 annually
Yield on Current Purchase Offer:	7.5%

Estimate of Value:	Property value:	*(in $1,000's)*	46,678
	R.E. commission @ 3%		(1,400)
	Mortgage notes payable		(17,720)
	Joint venture share		(0)
	Property equity		27,558
	Current assets		696
	Partnership equity		28,254
	Estimated GP share		(2,388)
	Total limited partner equity	*(in $1,000's)*	25,866
Current Value per L.P. Unit:	Divide by 30,000 LP units	=	**$862 per unit**

Discount from Current Value:	41%
Purchase Offer Price:	**$507 per unit**

Summary: Six of the properties are located in Southern California. The strong track record combined with good locations position these properties to well to fully realizing the benefits of an economic recovery. The result should be an increase in the value of these properties as the economy pulls out of the recession.

Because so many private partnerships exist and public information on them is so hard to come by, most dealers don't maintain active files on them. (Private partnerships which comply with the SEC's Regulation D are exempt from registration and reporting requirements, so SEC registration and public financial documents are unavailable.) When a limited partner in a private placement calls a dealer firm to express an interest in selling units, the firm will typically request that the partner directly send as much information on the partnership as he or she has available (i.e., quarterly and annual reports, the investor's most recent K-1 tax information, etc.).

RISK EVALUATION

A buyer of units in the secondary market should evaluate several important risks before signing a purchase contract. As discussed above, certain risks can be quantified by carefully looking at the partnership structure and its joint-venture agreements. Then there are the risks inherent in placing one's trust in the general partners by assuming ownership of the limited partnership units. How much experience do the general partners have? Do they have enough financial strength to help the partnership along, through a loan or cash advance, for example, if the need should arise?

Other risks require an acute awareness of local markets to evaluate. For instance, assume a partnership owns a number of office buildings in Atlanta, and the Atlanta office market that has 1 million square feet of office space currently under development that will come onto the market over the next 12 months. How is Atlanta faring in climbing out of the current recession compared to other market areas? If recovery is relatively slow, demand for office space will lag behind the increase in supply, property owners will find themselves in competition for lessees and will probably lower rents to attract new tenants. The effect might be to induce large tenant rollovers, causing many property owners, including the partnership, to experience a significant loss of revenue.

The smart buyer has to examine these issues under the light of current and projected economic conditions in order to determine what price, if any, should be paid for the units. If a partnership's office building remained vacant for two years, would the partnership be able to maintain it and survive until market conditions improved, or would the property be lost through foreclosure? Does any one property account for a significant percentage of the overall portfolio? How much would poor performance at one or two of the properties affect the overall partnership cash flow? Would the dividend be reduced? Eliminated? Answering such questions adequately may take a great deal of research and analytical expertise.

A dealer analyst will look at these factors and then make a number of assumptions—essentially educated guesses about what is likely to occur over the short term to intermediate term. For instance, for the real estate limited partnership exposed to a potentially soft rental market in Atlanta, the analyst may assume that the dividend will be suspended forever in order to keep the assets afloat. The analyst may further project that the properties will be held for an additional seven years (enough time for the market to turn around and appreciate substantially), at which time they would be sold for what they are worth today. If the break-up value for current liquidation were determined to be $600 per unit, the discounted price—based on the performance assumptions described above—may fall out at $200. Analysts never set out to arbitrarily determine a discount rate; they simply make educated estimates of key variables to determine a reasonable price to pay.

THE "INCOME-TO-DISCOUNT" CURVE

Unit pricing derives from the basic market forces of supply and demand. Supply and demand, in turn, are influenced by a host of factors, including the current yield provided by the units, the perceived current and future value of the assets and the risk associated with the investment, all of which are reflected in a price that usually results in a discount from break-up value per unit. Additionally, to a certain extent, pricing varies with the services provided by the firm that performs the research and effects the transaction on behalf of the buyer. To the extent that an investment is producing low levels of current income, the market tends to demand a higher discount to compensate for the lack of current return and the risk of waiting for deferred returns.

The graph shown in Figure 4.6 illustrates the inverse relationship between the discount and current yield (distributions from actual operating cash flow, *not* distributions from cash reserves). Simply stated, the higher the partnership's current yield, the lower the discount will be. At a 10 percent current yield, for example, an all-cash income real estate unit might sell at a discount of 10 percent from the analyst's estimated current break-up value per unit. A partnership with little or no current yield, say one in leveraged real estate, may be discounted up to

FIGURE 4.6 Secondary Market Discount-to-Yield Relationships

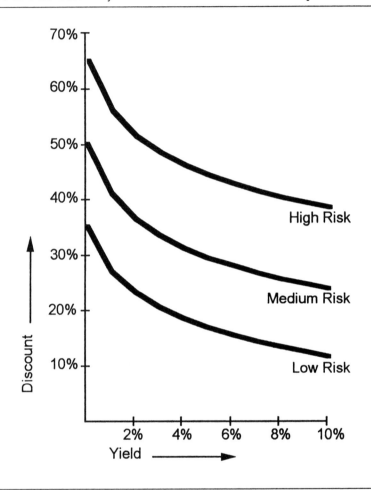

50 percent or more from estimated break-up value per unit. In other words, if a buyer wants to obtain the greatest amount of current income possible, he or she will have to "pay up" for it; the units that deliver the highest yield command the highest prices relative to the other types of units available in the market-place.

The income-to-discount curve also shifts based on supply and demand in the secondary market. With fewer buyers participating in the market, the curve will shift to the right, reflecting the fact that discount levels have to rise to compete for buyers. Similarly, when the number of buyers moving into the market increases, the curve will shift to the left, showing that investors are accepting lower yields and paying higher prices (i.e., accepting lower discounts) to compete for the more limited supply of available units.

The low-income spectrum of the secondary market has much deeper discounts from current asset values built into its pricing structure. For this reason, the long-term investor who doesn't demand high current income can acquire a higher multiple of equity per dollar invested. Moreover, there is a wider selection of partnership units with fewer buyers competing for them. Greater supply and lower demand skews the dollar-to-equity ratio even higher. The end result is that at the high-income end of the spectrum, each dollar invested may buy, for example, $1.10 of equity, while at the growth (i.e., low-current-yield) end, each dollar may buy $1.40 or more of equity, depending on the leverage and assessed risk of a given partnership.

LEVERAGE

In the secondary market for real estate partnership units, valuation and pricing are closely related to the amount of leverage the entity has used to purchase properties. The higher the leverage, the lower the current yield, because the more leveraged a partnership is, the higher the percentage of its operational cash flow goes to debt service. High leverage also increases the risk that income shortfalls in down markets can force a foreclosure, at worst, or refinancings at less attractive terms. These steps, in turn, can dilute the value of the owner's equity. Consequently, for a leveraged real estate partnership, the seller must allow a discount from break-up value great enough to offset the absence of current income and the increased risk of the investment.

Of course, leverage can also have a very positive effect on a real estate investment as is shown in Figure 4.7. Assume that you purchase a piece of real estate for $1 million, with a 25 percent down payment ($250,000) and a loan for 75 percent ($750,000).

FIGURE 4.7 Leverage

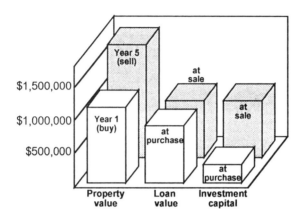

- A $1 million property is purchased with $250,000 of investment capital and a $750,000 loan.

- After five years it is sold for $1.5 million.

- The $750,000 loan is paid off, leaving the investor $750,000, three times the original investment (a 3 to 1 return) even though the value of the property has increased only 50%.

- If the same property were purchased with all cash ($1 million) and sold for the same price ($1.5 million) the return on investment would have been only 1.5 to 1. This is why, in a rising market, leverage can be very profitable.

Leveraged Investment

Year 1 (Purchase)	Year 5 (Sale)
Property value: 1,000,000	Property value: 1,500,000
Loan principal: 750,000	Loan principal: 750,000
Original investment: 250,000	Net proceeds to investor: 750,000

Return on investment: $750,000 / $250,000 = 3 to 1

All Cash Investment

Year 1 (Purchase)	Year 5 (Sale)
Property value: 1,000,000	Property value: 1,500,000
Loan principal: -0-	Loan principal: -0-
Original investment: 1,000,000	Net proceeds to investor: 1,500,000

Return on investment: $1,500,000 / $1,000,000 = 1.5 to 1

Further assume that within five years of your purchase, the property appreciates in value and you sell it for $1.5 million. After retiring the debt, you are left with approximately $750,000 in cash. You have earned 200 percent on your initial cash investment—you get three dollars back for every dollar invested—even though the value of the property went up only 50 percent. If you had bought the same property without any leverage, you would have received only a 50 percent return on each dollar invested. Another way of looking at all-cash ownership is that you have tied up four times as much money ($1 million versus $250,000) to get the same $500,000 profit. So when it works right—that is, when the value of a leveraged property goes up—the effect of leveraging is to lower the need for cash and thereby multiply investment return.

CONSERVATIVE INVESTMENT STRATEGY

The income-to-discount curve gets adjusted up or down depending on different variables, including leverage, current income, market risks and growth potential. Two partnerships with secondary market units selling at 25 percent discounts, for example, are not necessarily similar investments. One may be for a partnership that provides high current yield but owns properties in a softening rental market, while the other may be for a partnership with minimal current income but strong potential for equity growth.

Discounts of 50 percent are typical for leveraged, growth-oriented real estate units with little or no current income. The discount can climb as high as 75 percent for high-risk units. At the other end of the spectrum there are low leverage, all-cash real estate partnerships, with current yields running up to 10 percent, that are perceived as low risk investments. Many buyers opt for the maximum yield because they want income in their portfolio and feel most comfortable about the investment knowing that they will be getting a regular dividend check. As a result, they are buying units at the high current yield end of the curve, where they get the least discount. They believe that in seeking current income, they are taking the most conservative investment route, and they are, so long as they have done the research to assure that their dividends will not be cut.

But what these investors may fail to realize is that by insisting on maximum current income and paying top dollar (that is, buying at the low end of the discount curve, at or near the break-up value per unit), they are forfeiting the ability to get a more attractive discount from asset value and significant capital appreciation. They will not realize any substantially greater return if the assets appreciate. Moreover, they do not have the equity cushion that helps protect deep discount investors against a decline in asset values.

Thus, even conservative investors are sometimes better off not aiming for the highest-income partnership units, but buying into the market around the middle of the curve. Here they can obtain an adequate dividend—typically 6 percent or 7 percent–but still get the downside protection (and upside potential) of a substantial discount.

THE HIGH DISCOUNT INVESTMENT STRATEGY

At the heavily discounted, high leverage end of the curve, aggressive buyers can do well. Even if the real estate units don't appreciate in value, buying the units at a 40 percent to 50 percent discount means an investor stands to make 40 percent to 50 percent right off the top as the assets sell. And if the assets appreciate only a small amount, the leverage characteristic of many partnerships selling in the higher discount ranges can further boost this return. For instance, if a partnership's property was purchased with 75 percent leverage (three dollars of debt for every dollar of equity), 5 percent general inflation in a market's real estate values translates into a 15 percent annual growth rate for the owners' equity, giving the investor three-to-one leveraged return on the investment's growth.

In a down market, a deep discount works in the buyer's favor, too, as Figure 4.8 shows. If the units are purchased at a sizable discount (say, 40 percent to 50 percent from break-up value), and the assets decrease by 3 percent to 5 percent a year for several years because of unstable market conditions, the investor can

FIGURE 4.8 How Deep Discount Purchases of Leveraged Assets Enhance Return
in a Rising Market and Protect Principal in a Falling Market

The Effect of Purchasing 60% Leveraged Assets at a 50% Discount in a Market Rising at 5%/year

	Year 1	Year 2	Year 3	Year 4	Year 5	Year 6
Property Value	1,000,000	1,050,000	1,102,500	1,157,625	1,215,506	1,276,282
Loan Value	600,000	600,000	600,000	600,000	600,000	600,000
Current Break-up Value	400,000	450,000	502,500	557,625	615,506	676,282
Discounted Purchase Price	200,000	200,000	200,000	200,000	200,000	200,000
Gross Profit If Property Is Sold	200,000	250,000	302,500	357,625	415,506	476,282
Percent Return	100%	125%	151%	179%	208%	238%

The Effect of Purchasing 60% Leveraged Assets at a 50% Discount in a Market Declining at 3%/year

	Year 1	Year 2	Year 3	Year 4	Year 5	Year 6
Property Value	1,000,000	970,000	940,900	912,673	885,293	858,734
Loan Value	600,000	600,000	600,000	600,000	600,000	600,000
Current Break-up Value	400,000	370,000	340,900	312,673	285,293	258,734
Discounted Purchase Price	200,000	200,000	200,000	200,000	200,000	200,000
Gross Profit If Property Is Sold	200,000	170,000	140,900	112,673	85,293	58,734
Percent Return	100%	85%	70%	56%	43%	29%

The deep discounts from current asset value available in the secondary market for limited partnerships provide substantially increased profits in a rising market and offer a significant margin of safety, even if there is a long decline in real estate values over several years.

still break even, while the investor who purchased units at an undiscounted price will have lost principal. For the patient investor willing to take a little more risk and wait out bad markets, buying units at the high discount end of the curve can yield substantial long-term profits.

The high discount end, in fact, is where most of the pooled funds are invested. The majority of individual investors buy into the market around the middle of the curve, where the risks are fewer, and the potential rewards are also correspondingly smaller, but more certain.

In sum, when evaluating the potential rewards of pre-owned real estate units and developing a secondary market investment strategy, buyers need to concurrently consider all components of the investment: the discount, yield, risk and potential. Before buying, you should understand how current income and leverage affect discounting, and how discounts can not only mitigate risk, but also increase long-term gains potential. The ability to acquire assets at sixty cents on the dollar is a unique benefit of secondary market investing, and should not be overlooked by investors whose goal is long-term asset growth.

POOLED FUND INVESTING

An investor who participates in the secondary market by investing in a pooled fund must evaluate an additional factor: the fund's front-end fee that pays for organizational costs. A fund that buys units at a 50 percent discount but charges fees amounting to 40 percent of the investor's original capital passes on to the investor on a net discount of only 10 percent on the break-up value of units. The fund that buys units at a 50 percent discount and charges 20 percent in fees will pass a net 30 percent discount on to the investor.

Of course, a net 10 percent discount still may be economically worthwhile, depending on the particular units; nowhere is it written that discounts have to be above a certain level for a buyer to do well. It is the total context in which the discount exists that is important; a discount is meaningful only in the context of also evaluating the partnership units' yield, risk and growth potential. Although the pooled fund approach may result in smaller net discounts than a savvy secondary market shopper might achieve working individually through a knowledgeable broker or planner, pooled funds may well have substantially lower risk and higher growth potential than an individual secondary market investment. When you understand how some pooled funds are organized and managed, you can see why this may be so.

Return on Investment Modeling

Some of the more sophisticated dealers sponsor pooled funds organized around the concept that predetermined investment goals actually set the prices they are willing to offer for partnership units. The partnerships picked by analysts as potentially good investments are often run through a computerized investment simulation model to decide the appropriate price to offer for their units. For example, a target return on investment of 15 percent may be put into the model. Then added are certain assumptions about the length of time a partnership will continue to hold its assets, the degree of growth that will occur, the amount of income that will be realized by the fund and the types of risks that are involved in the investment. When all is said and done, the model might then show that the fund would need to pay 40 percent less than that particular partnership's break-up value to achieve that goal. Another partnership with slightly different characteristics might end up with a higher or lower target discount to achieve the same investment result.

Because each partnership is being evaluated individually, analysts fine-tune the results based on additional risk factors or expectations that a computer model may not measure. These could include the prospect of an economic downturn in a particular market area or for a certain asset class in which the partnership owns assets. The analyst will increase or decrease the discount accordingly in order to strike an appropriate balance between potential risk and reward. Each partnership is unique. Consequently, no blanket pricing formula applies to all of them. The target discount gets applied on a case-by-case basis.

The end result of this modeling and individualized fine-tuning is an extraordinarily disciplined pricing and acquisition methodology that very few individual investors and their brokers have a way to emulate. Pooled funds can set their own unit pricing according to the investment return they seek. Once the pricing standards are set, the fund simply starts acquiring units as they become available from what are, in essence, preapproved and prepriced partnerships.

Taking Advantage of Supply and Demand Variations

In another sense, the pooled funds operate quite differently from traders in the open market in that they can take better advantage of supply and demand considerations. The majority of the partnerships traded by brokers on behalf of individual clients (as opposed to the much wider range of partnerships followed and acquired by the pooled funds) are comparable to blue chip stocks in that everyone in the market has heard of them, their performance is easy to follow and they represent the highest volume of trading. Discounts for such blue-chip units tend to be lower because demand for them is higher. With sophisticated research expertise constantly identifying new partnerships becoming available and an extensive data base of already-traded partnerships that they monitor, pooled funds are typically in a much better position than the individual broker to acquire units of equally valuable, but lesser known partnerships—for which there is little demand in the secondary market—or to acquire more widely followed partnerships at times when their discounts may rise because of a periodic slump in demand.

Diversification

Finally, pooled funds offer unparalleled diversification. On their own, investors may be able to spread risk by building a portfolio including units of five or ten different partnerships. For an equivalent, or perhaps much smaller investment commitment through a pooled fund, the same investor could spread his holdings over the 20 to 50 partnerships, representing ownership in several hundred individual properties! (See Figure 4.9.)

Well-managed pooled funds offer investors significant benefits—a disciplined pricing and acquisition methodology, access

FIGURE 4.9   Unique Features of Pooled Fund Investments in the Real Estate
Partnership Secondary Market

**(Funds sponsored by top market makers
have most or all of these features)**

*Selection of
Assets:* - A disciplined acquisition methodology that takes advantage of marketplace supply and demand by applying Return on Investment Modeling to a wide selection of thoroughly researched partnerships.

Management: - Professional managers monitor performance of every partnership owned by the fund.

Diversification:
- 20 - 50 partnerships
- 50 - 75 markets
- Wide variety of program types
- Up to several hundred individual properties

(Compare with an individual investor:
- single partnership
- 4 - 10 markets
- 1 - 3 program types
- 10 - 20 properties)

Taxation - Diversification permits blending of fund assets for tax-neutral effect.

*Annual Tax
Report ("K-1"):*
- Only one K-1 (delayed until last partnership reports to fund managers)
- Estimated K-1 sent well before tax-filing time

*Suitability
Requirements:* Any number of accredited investors:
- $1 million net worth, or
- Annual income of $200,000), or
- Net worth of 5 times investment, if investment is $150,000 or more

Up to 99 Non-accredited Investors

*Minimum
Investment:* $25,000 - $50,000

---

to a wider selection of partnerships, an edge in achieving substantial discounts from break-up value (which offset fees changed to perform services such as research), extraordinary diversification and professional management—that make them well worth considering as a strategic investment vehicle.

Clearly, investing in the secondary market for limited partnership interests is not like buying CDs. A high level of investment sophistication is a prerequisite for this market. An objective, analytical evaluation of a secondary market investment takes a great deal of research and time. Prospective buyers and their brokers must feel comfortable evaluating and discussing partnership cash flow, underlying asset value, sharing arrangements, equity risks and current versus sustainable yields. They also need a well-founded strategy for determining discounted prices based on these factors.

Individual investors should either make use of a pooled fund that provides a professionally managed portfolio of assets or seek the help of a broker, planner or secondary partnership dealer that can supply the analytical services on an individual trading basis. Whether an investor chooses the pooled investment approach or seeks to build a portfolio on his or her own, it is advisable to enlist the services of an experienced secondary market firm to help with the investment selection.

CHAPTER 5

Taxation and Regulation

Investors and securities representatives trading in secondary limited partnership interests are well advised to have an overview of a series of securities and tax regulations that have a substantial impact on the nature of the market. Various changes in tax laws in the seventies created the fundamental playing field for limited partnerships as a form of investment that allowed the pass-through of tax benefits. Limited partnerships flourished in the early and mid-eighties in part because lackluster stockmarket performance in the seventies and double-digit inflation made real estate look great. However, another significant factor was the 1981 Tax Act, which significantly improved the tax benefits of real estate, equipment leasing and other depreciable investments. The same act created IRAs, an investment account that had to be long-term and seemed ideally suited for limited partnerships. The 1986 Tax Reform Act, however, made fundamental changes in partnership tax advantages that cut short the growth of the limited partnership sector of the securities industry. At the same time the 1986 act gave impetus to the growth of the secondary market; after the loss of significant tax advantages, the number of limited partners who wanted to liquidate their units increased.

As the secondary market has expanded, the need for specialized rules and regulations has grown more apparent. For these reasons, an overview of the securities law and regulatory agencies governing trading in this market is essential to understanding its history and origins, key taxation and securities issues, the extent of investor protection, and how the market's future may be shaped by regulations currently being proposed or debated.

CONSUMER PROTECTION

The securities industry is highly regulated and closely watched by several regulatory agencies at the federal, state and industry level, each of which serves to reinforce the efforts of the others. Any secondary market trades are securities trades and, as such, are subject to the same rules, regulations and guidelines as any other securities trade.

The Securities Act of 1933 put several tiers of regulation in place to protect investors. The 1933 act is sometimes referred to as the "paper act" because it regulates the securities themselves (i.e., the stocks, bonds and partnership units). It requires all securities issuers to:

- make full and fair disclosure about the nature of the securities being offered;
- not commit fraud, not make a material misstatement in describing the securities, nor omit a material fact;
- for publicly offered securities, file a registration statement with the SEC and periodically update it during the time when the securities are being sold;
- provide investors with a prospectus outlining the terms of the investment; and
- after a public security is sold, file regular financial reports.

Securities industry regulations further govern the activities of the broker-dealer firms that trade in partnership secondary market units. Broker-dealers who buy and sell securities are subject to a wide array of licensing, financial reporting, accounting, client communication and minimum reserve requirements, and operate under the surveillance of several regulatory agencies.

At the federal level, the Securities and Exchange Commission (SEC) has established a set of rules and regulations that define the manner in which brokers can conduct operations under the Securities Exchange Act of 1934, also known as the "people act" (as opposed to the 1933 "paper act"). The 1934 act regulates the activities of brokers and firms in the securities industry. Most importantly, the 1934 act mandates that anyone selling a security must be licensed to do so. The SEC can enforce its rules by: censuring a broker's activities; restricting the areas in which a broker does business; suspending a broker's business for a period of up to 12 months; or, as a last measure, revoking the broker's registration.

The states, too, have their own securities laws and regulatory agencies to enforce them; in California, a representative example, the Commissioner of Corporations, Securities Division, monitors the operations of brokerage firms that conduct business within its jurisdiction. Reporting rules and regulations differ from state to state. Consequently, a broker-dealer may have to prepare a number of different types of reports to comply with the requirements of the different states in which it sells securities.

The securities exchanges to which a brokerage firm belongs, such as the NYSE, the AMEX, the Chicago Board of Trade, etc., also have standards of conduct. And, finally, the National Association of Securities Dealers (NASD) serves as a self-regulatory agency for securities brokerage firms to (1) act as an intermediary between brokers and governmental agencies, (2) adopt and promote rules of fair practice and (3) ensure that the operations of its constituent members are ethical and above-board.

All these securities regulation frameworks are designed to create an even playing field in the marketplace, and to protect investors from the extraordinary problems that might arise from, for example, insolvent brokerage firms or unlicensed brokers. Nonetheless, no securities regulations can truly protect consumers from making unwise investments. In any investment—but especially investments in a security as complicated to evaluate as secondary market partnership units—it is up to the individual investor to make certain that he or she is dealing with a reputable, reliable and experienced broker or dealer firm, and to make no investment without first fully understanding the potential risks involved.

THE TAX REFORM ACT OF 1986

Perhaps the greatest single impact in recent years on the health of savings and loan institutions, insurance companies and certainly, partnership investments resulted from the Tax Reform Act of 1986. The TRA 1986 substantially affected investment taxation, property values and accounting costs—all negatively.

"Passive" Income and Investment Taxation

Before 1986, only two types of taxable income existed: ordinary income and capital gains. The 1986 reform created a third category, "passive income," necessitating a completely different kind of tax treatment. The restrictions on the uses of passive income and passive loss helped lessen demand for new real estate partnership offerings.

In the heyday of limited partnership investing, any taxable loss resulting from the operation of the partnership's assets could be used to offset income earned from any other source. The 1986 act brought this practice to a halt. Losses now classified as "passive" (i.e., those in which partners had no direct involvement) can be used only to offset income that is also "passively" earned. The trouble with this restriction lies in the definition of a passive activity. Even if a partnership owns the building on which it is making payments, and the building is losing money—on a real cash basis—those losses can no longer be used by the limited partners unless the partnership (or another passive investment the limited partners may have) owns another property that is generating passive income.

The application of this rule is particularly troublesome because although the limited partners may not actively participate in the management of the building, it is still their money being used to keep the building operational. For example, the property may be costing the partnership $100,000 per year to operate, but because of high vacancies, total rental income may be only $85,000, with the $15,000 difference representing the partnership's real negative cash flow to pay for the real expenses of keeping the building lighted, heated, cleaned, repaired, etc. Prior to 1986, limited partners could have used their proportionate share of that $15,000—plus noncash expenses, such as deprecia-tion—to offset any other type of income. Now they cannot do so. They can hold the loss and carry it forward to the time of the building's sale, using it at that time to offset any gain from the sale. But what if, when the building is sold, the partnership doesn't realize a gain? What if, because of poor market condi-tions, the sale results in a loss instead? In that event, the passive losses that were carried forward simply disappear, unless you can use them in the future to offset passive gains. (See Figure 5.1.)

Asset Devaluation

So here's the limited partnership, between the proverbial rock and a hard place, suffering a real $15,000 per year loss; the general partners may suspect that conditions won't improve in the near future, and they can't even realize any tax benefit from the loss. Can the owners command the same price for their piece of real estate as they might have before the deductibility of passive losses was lost? Clearly not, so the change in tax laws to reduce the deductibility of losses also caused the net value of many types of assets to fall. Real estate was the asset type hardest hit because investors typically used as much as 70 percent to 80 percent leverage, and when asset values fell, many properties were simply not worth enough to pay off their financing.

Consider the example of a hypothetical investor purchasing an office building in 1985. As part of the determination of paying, say, $1 million, the investor may have calculated that $250,000 was the value of the tax benefits that would result from owning the piece of income-producing real estate over the next few years. Eliminating the tax benefits in 1986 would have had the general effect of decreasing the value of the building to as low as $750,000. If the investor had purchased the building with 80 percent financing and 20 percent down, he would be left with an $800,000 mortgage on a building now worth only $750,000. In a situation like this, the incentive to stop making payments on the loan would have been great. And that, in fact, is precisely what a lot of borrowers did; they simply walked away from their loan obligations.

FIGURE 5.1   Effects of the 1986 Tax Reform Act on the Deductibility of
Losses and Property Values

	Pre-1986	Post-1986
Deductibility of Operating Expenses		
Investment operating expenses	$100,000	$100,000
Investment income	85,000	85,000
Loss	-15,000	-15,000
Percent deductible against earned income	100%	None
Asset Devaluation		
Purchase price	$1,000,000	$1,000,000
Present value of tax deductions over five years	250,000	0
Cash invested	200,000	200,000
Mortgage	800,000	800,000
Resale value	1,000,000	750,000
Resale value less mortgage	$200,000	($50,000)

It has been estimated that the 1986 act reduced the value of income real estate by as much as 20 percent. A property owner with a substantial mortgage faced two choices: continue making payments on a loan with a balance that exceeded the actual value of the property or shrug off the obligation and let the lender foreclose on the property. More and more, savings and loans found themselves stuck with income properties that they were ill-equipped to manage and for which they also had to book losses. The savings and loan that had funded an $800,000 loan on a property that was worth only $750,000 would have had to augment its own net capital to account for the difference.

Other types of assets were not affected quite as dramatically as real estate because the amount of financing used for their purchase had been less. A leveraged equipment purchase, for instance, typically consists of 65 percent to 70 percent debt. Nonetheless, these investment classes suffered as well.

Tax Reporting Expenses

Moreover, tax reporting complications created by the 1986 act drove another nail into the coffin of real estate partnership demand. The regulations concerning applicability of passive income and loss are so arcane and difficult to interpret that the average investor can no longer complete the federal returns alone without the help of an accountant or tax specialist. State returns are equally as complex, with individual returns now required in each state in which the partnership owns property. It has been estimated that the majority of limited partners who have struggled to complete their own returns have made mistakes in complying with new federal and state rules.

The limited partner's only recourse is to hire a professional, which further saps the value of the partnership investment. An individual who has $20,000 invested in a limited partnership and is receiving a 7 percent per annum return through distributions ($1,400 per year) now may have to pay $200 (to as much as $500 on complicated partnerships) to have a certified public accountant complete his tax returns for him. This decreases by $200 the return on his investment, from $1,400 per year to $1,200 per year. No wonder investor interest in new issues dried up, and why many existing investors wished to sell in the secondary market! In turn, this cost must be taken into account by the secondary market buyer. It is one of the reasons for the discounts demanded by buyers.

"SAFE HARBOR" LIMITS

Tax reform didn't end in 1986. In 1987 the Technical Corrections Act was enacted partly in response to fears about the disincorporation of the United States. Prior to then, some large corporations had changed to partnership status to avoid double taxation. A corporation pays income tax on corporate profits, then distributes the after-tax net earnings to shareholders, who pay income tax a second time on shareholder dividends. Limited partnerships, in themselves, do not have any tax obligations; all of the partnership's income and losses are passed through directly to limited partners. With limited partners instead of shareholders, the newly disincorporated businesses could pay no tax at the corporate level and pass more income to shareholders.

Congress was concerned that if all business entities had the ability to structure themselves as limited partnerships rather than corporations, a significant amount of tax revenue would be lost. To protect tax revenue, Congress created a new rule specifying that if too much liquidity existed for limited partnerships, for tax purposes they would be treated more like corporations. Specifically, as long as only a small percentage—5 percent or less—of a partnership's units are traded, the partnership is in a "safe harbor" with regard to its partnership status. If more than 5 percent of a partnership's units are traded within a given year, or if the partnership's units are traded on a securities exchange, it is no longer in the safe harbor. Partnerships out of safe harbor limitations are more likely to be deemed to have liquidity, like a publicly held corporation. This could cause the partnership's preferential tax status to be lost.

It is important to realize, however, that safe harbor rules do not really create any risk for limited partners. This is because the general partners control the transfer of units, and they certainly do not want to sail out of the safe harbor into the sea of corporate income taxes! The percentage of units currently being traded annually in the secondary market is quite low; very few partnerships have topped the 2 percent level and the great majority of commonly traded partnerships are at just a fraction of 1 percent. If the percentage ever nears the 5 percent limit in a given year, you can be certain the general partners will simply stop booking transfers until next January 1.

PRIVATE (REGULATION D) PARTNERSHIPS

Certain securities are, by nature, exempt from the SEC's registration requirements, which dictate that a registration and prospectus first be filed with the SEC. These exempt securities include government bonds and short-term commercial paper. Other securities merit exemption based on the type of transaction involved in the offering. For example, under Regulation D of Section 4(2) of the 1933 act, an issuer that offers securities privately is exempt from registering the securities with the SEC. Regulation D provides the specific guidelines for such private offerings (also called private placements) within which issuers can claim the exemption from the filing requirements of the 1933 act. Conforming to Regulation D ensures that the private placement will be exempt.

A key restriction of Regulation D offerings is that they can have no more than 35 nonaccredited investors but may have an unlimited number of accredited investors. Accredited investors are defined in several ways: (1) individuals having substantial net worth ($1 million or more); (2) those earning high income (at least $200,000 for the two years preceding investment, with the anticipation of equivalent income in the current year); (3) those who invest $150,000 or more, providing that the total investment doesn't exceed 20 percent of the investor's net worth; (4) insiders, such as directors, executive officers and general partners; and (5) institutions, such as banks, insurance companies, pension and employee benefit plans, and certain large nonprofit organizations.

Regulation D requirements are significant because the same minimum acceptability standards also apply to purchasers of privately placed partnership units in the secondary market. In other words, if a limited partnership is originally issued as a Regulation D private placement for accredited investors, only investors documenting that they meet the same suitability standards may purchase units that are being sold in the secondary market. For this reason, the pooled investment funds have high minimum net worth and minimum income standards, since every one of the limited partners of a pooled fund must meet the minimum suitability standards of any partnership in which the fund purchases units.

CAPITAL RESERVE REQUIREMENTS AND THE "NET CAPITAL BURDEN"

In the area of minimum capital reserves, SEC regulations governing securities dealers were understandably not designed in full contemplation of the relatively new secondary market for partnership units. This fact limits the number of firms participating in the market and increases the cost of transactions. Under the 1934 act, the SEC requires that every brokerage firm maintain certain minimum net capital reserves (very much akin to net worth, but with some special adjustments), which vary depending on the nature of the broker-dealer's business, the types of securities traded and the size of the firm. After subtracting the broker-dealer's aggregate liabilities from aggregate capital, if the firm does not show sufficient net capital to meet its minimum requirement, the broker-dealer must reach into its own pocket to augment the account.

Aggregate capital is defined as all the capital owned by the firm, less certain items for which the SEC won't allow full or even partial credit. For example, among these items are bonds with long maturity dates. The more extended the maturity date, the less credit is available to the broker; only a certain percentage of the bonds' value is permitted to be included in aggregate capital. For instance, if the broker-dealer holds bonds that have a face value of $1,000 in ten years, but their current trading value is $450, the broker-dealer can at least apply $450 to its aggregate capital account.

In contrast, because limited partnership units do not have a "public market" with standardized trades (the buy/sell offers listed by individual dealer firms do not constitute a public market), they are considered illiquid and are valued at zero for purposes of computing net capital under SEC rules. The result? A market-making broker-dealer that buys them has to suffer a 100 percent "haircut" to its net capital. When $100 is paid out to purchase limited partnership units, the brokerage firm has to come up with an additional $100 to replace it in its net capital account.

Aggregate capital also excludes another item that would normally be included in a normal book value computation of capital.

A broker-dealer typically has commissions receivable and payable. In calculating book value, the firm's payables are deducted from receivables to generate a net payables number. Not so in calculating net capital. Commissions receivable get no credit whatsoever; commissions payable, however, are added 100 percent into aggregate indebtedness. The logic behind this conservative approach to valuation is that if the entity owing the commissions to the broker-dealer defaulted on its obligation to pay, the broker-dealer would lose a current asset but would still be obligated to pay out the commissions it owed to its own representatives and affiliates.

Thus, after buying a limited partnership interest for cash and before reselling it, the market-making broker-dealer may find itself saddled with an "asset" that represents a 100 percent deduction from aggregate capital. Many small brokers can't afford to take the big hit to their net capital that participating in the secondary market may demand. The bigger dealers who do participate in the market certainly take the net capital "haircut" into consideration when making valuations and purchasing decisions. Undeniably, this regulatory anomaly creates an extra cost of capital that is a factor in every dealer purchase. (See Figure 5.2.) The dealer must pay the seller less, charge the buyer more or both to make up for this extra cost, so its elimination would be a clear benefit to investors.

The simplest solution to this net capital burden would be to develop a more structured secondary market for limited partnerships, including a trading floor and a display similar to the NASD Automated Quotation System (NASDAQ). NASDAQ is a computerized communications system that collects, stores and displays up-to-the-second quotations from a network of broker-dealers. The system serves as an instantaneous electronic link between the major retail firms and over-the-counter dealer. What makes NASDAQ so valuable is that it enables the best market for a given security to be located instantly, regardless of its location. Because each dealer can see competitors' quotations, price spreads and markups tend to shrink. A NASDAQ-type display system would cause trading volume in the partnership secondary market to increase. Thus, a ready market for partnership units would be deemed to exist, and, consequently, the units

FIGURE 5.2   Capital Reserves and the Net Capital Burden

	Dealer in NYSE Stocks	Dealer in R.E. Secondary Market
Capitalization	$5,000,000	$5,000,000
Securities purchased with cash	3,000,000	3,000,000
Remaining cash	2,000,000	2,000,000
Amount of securities applied to minimum net aggregate capital	$1,800,000	$0
Net aggregate capital	$3,800,000	$2,000,000

The effects of the *net capital burden* on secondary market dealers:
• Decreases inventory that can be held
• Decreases the volume of trading a firm can undertake
• Increases the cost of capital relative to the volume of transactions

could be credited to a broker's net capital. Today, largely because of inadequate information flow, many limited partnerships have no secondary market at all. The bulk of the trading in the partnership aftermarket involves only a small percentage of all the limited partnerships that exist.

However, as securities and tax laws currently stand, the development of an exchange or trading floor for limited partnership units might threaten the limited partner status of all partnership investors, so some regulatory revisions may be needed before investors and brokers can enjoy the advantages of such an easily accessed quotation system.

"PHANTOM GAIN" TAX AND THE SECTION 754 ELECTION

Another reason why partnership units sell at a discount is potential tax liability. The most significant potential liability is that as a buyer, you assume the tax basis of the original investor, unless the general partner has granted the so-called Section 754 election, which seldom occurs. In effect, this means the buyer must pay the tax liability on the depreciation already taken by the seller. If you are going to pay a tax liability on "phantom gain" that you have never received, you are certainly going to discount the units by enough to cover that liability.

General partners can elect to make an adjustment in the partnership's accounting—the Section 754 election—that makes it possible for buyers to avoid assuming the seller's low tax basis. Certainly such an accounting change will result in administrative and accounting costs. This is one reason why general partners typically do not take the Section 754 election, since neither they, nor the partnership, nor limited partners who choose not to sell units derive any benefit from the election. However, in large partnerships the cost is *de minimus* for the partnership and provides an attractive benefit of increased liquidity for limited partners.

In fact, if general partners take the election, the net effect is to increase the liquidity and the secondary market value of their limited partners' units, since buyers no longer have to discount for a tax liability on phantom gain. Will higher valuation and readier salability increase the number of limited partners choosing to sell their partnership interests? In all likelihood, yes. Since most general partners prefer not to see limited partners cashing out—the discounted prices could make the partnership look bad and encourage even more limited partners to sell—they really have little motivation to take the Section 754 election.

"MARKUP"—HOW MUCH IS JUSTIFIED?

A "markup" is the increase in price that a securities firm creates in a riskless transaction—that is, when a firm acts as an agent, buying securities on behalf of a client and reselling them immediately to the client. In a transaction involving risk, when the broker acts as a dealer and actually purchases the security for its own account before finding a buyer with the intention of holding it in inventory and reselling it at an unknown future date, the difference between the purchase and sales prices is referred to as the "spread," and is not subject to the same limitations. In a transaction in which the broker simply acts as an intermediary, however, and does not place any of its own capital at risk, the difference between the purchase and sales prices is deemed to be a markup. According to the NASD Rules of Fair Practice, the amount of markup charged by a brokerage firm in effecting a traditional over-the-counter (OTC) securities transaction should typically be 5 percent or less, unless other unusual costs are incurred or services provided. This is known as the 5 percent guideline.

Questions have arisen as to exactly what level markups taken in the secondary partnership market are fair. Is there justification for a brokerage firm to mark up secondary market partnership securities substantially more than the traditional 5 percent guideline? Think for a moment what is involved in buying or selling an OTC stock as an agent for a client. The securities representative looks up the security on a computerized listing that provides up-to-the-minute buy and sell quotes, checks with the client to see if the price is acceptable and completes the transaction by filling out a simple trading ticket. Now assume that a particular customer wants to buy 20 units (originally $1,000 per unit) of a thinly traded limited partnership. The representative cannot simply pull up a listing on a NASDAQ-type screen or call a representative at a major securities exchange to see what is available. The representative's firm has to actively search for those units, unless, by chance, the firm happens to have a quantity of them sitting in its securities box. Hunting for the units may involve substantial time and effort, and may include contacting the general partner to see if they have any potential sellers listed, or contacting a number of limited partners directly to see if any potential sales exist, then negotiating a price.

Further, once the firm finds the sought-after units, the lengthy process of transferring title begins. Stock trading on a major securities exchange is so electronically streamlined that the shares normally are not physically delivered to the purchaser. Instead, the National Securities Clearing Corporation continually debits and credits brokerage accounts for each completed buy and sell transaction. Thus in one central location it consolidates and vastly simplifies brokers' bookkeeping obligations. With this speedy, automated system, accounts are settled at the end of each day.

Not so in the partnership secondary market. Weeks and months may go by between the time the units are bought and when they are actually delivered to the purchaser, during which time the brokerage firm must continuously track the progress of the transfer of ownership. Simply, there is no standardization of transfer procedures. This means that in some transactions, the buying or selling broker must implement the entire transfer process. In other cases, a market-making broker-dealer will take care of most of the details for the broker. Thus, no "standard" markup exists in the partnership aftermarket, and they can legitimately range up to 7 percent or more.

Clearly, the nature of the market in which the securities are being traded, the availability of the securities, or the extent of services required of the broker must be allowed for. Considering the actual complexities and expenses of completing a partnership unit transfer, it is easy to see that the cost of the transaction is totally unrelated to the cost of buying or selling stocks or bonds on the major exchanges. Markups in excess of the 5 percent guideline can indeed be fair.

In fact, since trading secondary market partnership units involves extraordinary costs, markups high enough to cover expenses are not only justified, but necessary. Without adequate markups, brokerage firms would be unwilling to make the transactions, sellers would be unable to liquidate their partnership holdings and buyers would not have access to the investment opportunities the market offers.

DEALER "SPREADS"

When a broker-dealer buys partnership units for immediate resale to an identified client, the firm is acting as a "riskless principal." In accordance with NASD regulations, the markup it places on the units must be limited to fairly reflect the firm's transaction costs, plus a reasonable profit. When a market-making broker-dealer buys partnership units to hold as inventory in its own account, a different set of guidelines come into play. Article III, Section 4, of the NASD Rules of Fair Practice provides that:

> In over-the-counter transactions, whether in "listed" or "unlisted" securities, if a member buys for his own account from his customer, or sells for his own account to his customer, he shall buy or sell at a price which is fair, taking into consideration all relevant circumstances, including market conditions with respect to such security at the time of the transaction, the expense involved, and the fact that he is entitled to a profit.

NASD regulators are generally applying the guidelines for dealer spreads to the partnership secondary market in the same way they are applied to broker-dealers who deal in stocks and bonds. The partnership secondary market is such a new industry that regulators do not yet fully understand it. To treat partnership interest transfers the same as stock and bond transactions is an error due to a lack of understanding of the unique features of the partnership market. Dealers involved in the partnership area are making an effort to educate regulators about the unique nature of this market.

Most standard securities transactions in the United States clear within five days; the majority of secondary market partnership transactions do not clear after 30 days to as long as 90 days. A dealer who buys partnership units enters a lengthy and cumbersome process involving preparation of transfer documents, accounting, follow-ups and securities counts that would never be required in the course of a more traditional securities transaction.

Moreover, as we have pointed out, the dealer also assumes a net capital burden, since the asset value of the partnership units are excluded from reserve capital calculations. The cost of capital in the secondary market is extraordinarily high because cash must be paid out to purchase the units, then additional cash must be set aside to meet minimum reserve requirements.

Then there is the risk of guaranteed distributions, which some dealers assume. Any partnership distributions occurring after the date the units are purchased legitimately belong to the buyer.

But because of delays of up to 90 days before a transfer is entered in the general partner's books, distributions are commonly made to the seller, even after he or she may have received full payment for the units. To facilitate the sale of units, some dealers guarantee distributions, automatically paying buyers out-of-pocket an amount equal to any distributions, and assuming the risk of collecting the distribution from the seller.

Consider also the time and expense that go into analyzing and evaluating partnerships prior to purchase, and into maintaining updated information on all partnerships in inventory. Clearly, dealers provide an important service to both sellers and buyers by 1) providing analytical services which help establish valuation for the marketplace, 2) maintaining an inventory of partnership units, which creates liquidity for both buyers and sellers, and 3) assuming liability and expense for the cumbersome task of transferring ownership. Just as clearly, the extra time and paperwork entailed in providing these services generate substantial additional costs compared to maintaining inventory and effecting transfer in the secondary market for stocks and bonds.

Artificially limiting the spread in this market will have two effects: it will drive some dealers out of the business and it will prevent others from entering into smaller trades. The end result will be to decrease liquidity for people who wish to sell their units and to limit access to the market to the biggest players. Fixed costs are associated with every transaction, whether it is a $2,000 trade or a $20,000 trade. The cost of transferring units has to be allocated on a per-transaction basis. Say spreads are capped at 10 percent and the fixed cost of transferring a trade is $200. If a $2,000 transaction costs a dealer $200, there is no profit, so $2,000 transactions simply will not be made. Only much larger transactions will be feasible, so only big-time investors will have access to the market. Consider an investor with a small limited partnership holding who is perfectly willing to sell at a 40 percent discount and another small investor more than happy to buy at a 15 percent discount. With a limit on spreads, a dealer simply will not be able to make the transaction, and both small investors will be prevented from achieving their goals.

Over time, if limited partners are to achieve maximum liquidity at the highest prices, the unique aspects and costs must be recognized. This is inevitable, yet it is still understandable why it is slow in coming.

STATE BLUE-SKY REGULATIONS

When a new security is issued, it must not only comply with SEC securities regulations, but also with regulations of each state in which it is to be sold. The process of acquiring certification on a state-by-state basis that compliance requirements have been met is known as "blue skying" a new issue security.

The term *blue sky* comes from the basic intent of most state securities regulations. Unlike the SEC, which is only concerned with the full and fair disclosure of information, the states are concerned with preventing someone from selling the "blue sky above" without any substantive (or merit) basis for the securities offering. Hence, regulations in many states impose a fairness test to securities transactions based upon a set of standards which many states have adopted in concert. In fact, for partnerships, most states have adopted the guidelines of the North American Securities Administrators Association (NASAA), the organization composed of the securities departments in all 50 states.

However, after a security has been issued to original investors, the states have vastly different regulations regarding secondary trades, as Figure 5.3 shows. In New York and Washington, D.C., for example, there are no limitations to secondary securities transactions between any two parties. Some states, such as Colorado and Florida, require only that 10Ks and 10Qs must be filed with the state securities regulatory agency for secondary market securities to be traded. Others, including Michigan, Minnesota and North Dakota, require that the underlying corporation or partnership have a minimum annual income of $1 million. Some states, such as California and Texas, have particularly complicated rules and regulations regarding secondary market transactions.

The trouble with these various blue-sky regulations is that, as far as trading partnership units is concerned, they can be vague, ambiguous and quite haphazard. In most cases, it turns out that there simply are no regulations specific to a secondary market

FIGURE 5.3 Blue-Sky Clearance Overview

CLEAR ALL SECURITIES		CLEAR CERTAIN SECURITIES			RESTRICTED / PROHIBITED	
All Clear	Section 12 SEC Filings	"Blue Chip" Net Inc. > $1MM 4 of 5 years	Unrelated Person/No Stop Order	Previous Registration	Partially Restricted	Prohibited
D.C.	Alabama	Kansas	Delaware	Alaska	California*(1)	Connecticut
New York*(2)	Colorado	Michigan	Georgia*	Arizona	Texas (3)	Hawaii
	Florida	Minnesota	Louisiana*	Arkansas		Idaho
	Illinois	Montana*	Maryland	Indiana		Mississippi
	Iowa	Nebraska	Pennsylvania*	Kentucky*		New Jersey
	Maine	New Hampshire		Ohio		Rhode Island*
	Massachusetts	North Dakota		Oregon		South Carolina
	Missouri	Tennessee*		Washington		Utah
	Nevada	Wyoming				Vermont
	New Mexico					Virginia*
	North Carolina					West Virginia
	Oklahoma					
	South Dakota					
	Wisconsin*					

* No Manual Exemption Available

(1) California allows the purchase of limited partnership interest by broker-dealer firms and third parties. Clarification is being sought for application of statutes to agency trades.

(2) The New York securities division has indicated that it does not regulate the secondary market.

(3) Texas allows trading of interests in the secondary market if the issuer is registered in the state and meets the blue chip exemption, provided also that the issuer is a going concern.

for partnership interests, so partnership unit trades are again forced to comply with regulations originally designed for corporate securities. This problem is so significant that in 1991, some major dealer firms suspended taking orders for purchases of secondary market units from residents of eleven states—Connecticut, Hawaii, Idaho, Mississippi, New Jersey, Rhode Island, South Carolina, Utah, Vermont, Virginia and West Virginia—that have no clear exemption for partnership units from corporate blue-sky provisions. (This suspension does not extend to private-placement, or Regulation D offerings organized by dealers to invest in secondary market partnership units. Private placements are subject to a different set of blue-sky regulations, and typically continue to be offered in states where they previously were offered.)

Some adjustment of state blue-sky laws will be needed to increase the liquidity of limited partnership units. As the partnership secondary market develops, and as efforts to educate state regulatory agencies are made by those with an interest in the standardization and growth of the market, further guidelines will no doubt be developed and refined. The major market-making broker-dealers will no doubt be a prime mover in encouraging this process and in keeping investors and their brokers informed of its progress.

THE SEC PAPERWORK CONTROVERSY

To date, about half of the trades in the partnership resale market are made by "matching services" run by big securities firms, such as Merrill Lynch, PaineWebber, Prudential Securities, Dean Witter Reynolds, Shearson Lehman Brothers and others. They bring together sellers of partnerships those firms originally sold with buyers, who are also clients of the firm. The other half of the trades are made by independent firms that also act as matchmakers, or as dealers, buying and selling for their own accounts. These independents did not participate in the original offerings of any of the partnerships, but will trade in any partnership they believe will produce activity.

The existence of the Wall Street brokerage firm matching services has been threatened by a SEC directive issued in 1991 that would require the firms to continually update the prospectuses of some partnerships. Upset at the potential impact of this directive, these major brokerage firms launched a campaign to get the agency to rewrite the directive. According to a report in *The Wall Street Journal* (September 12, 1991), a spokesperson for Merrill Lynch said the SEC edict "may have unintended consequences on the liquidity of these partnership interests. We have commenced a dialogue with the SEC and intend to seek some clarifications."

The major brokerage firms, according to the *Journal* report, are not opposed to the directive by a reluctance to disclose bad news about old partnerships, but are concerned about high costs of carrying out the directive as it stands. Their complaint has considerable merit. One major brokerage firm estimates that updating a prospectus costs at least $100,000 in administrative, accounting and legal fees. Multiply that amount by the total number of partnerships involved in a firm's matching services, and you have an extraordinary increase in the cost of providing the service. Rather than incur these expenses for such a limited market, many firms would simply shut down their matching services.

If the SEC directive stands as originally written, liquidity for all but the largest partnerships serviced by brokerage house matching services will be affected. Ultimately, much of the slack might be taken up by the independent dealers, but until the independent firms had time to analyze and evaluate those partnerships, their buyers and sellers would be without access to a market.

HAVE REGULATIONS ENDED THE "ROLLUP" TREND?

In the mid-eighties an unfortunate trend started among partnership securities that hurt many investors and tarnished the image of the industry. "Rollups"—theoretically new investment entities formed by "rolling up" several existing limited partnerships into a new "master" security, typically a partnership or real estate investment trust (REIT)— in fact became an overriding threat to the secondary market and certainly were a significant factor in depressing prices for secondary units.

Why were rollups so bad? For several reasons. First, if you had partnership interests in a successful, well-managed partnership, and it was "rolled up" with a bunch of losers, you immediately became a loser, too. The averaging effect on valuation inherent to rollups is categorically unfair to investors in all the partnerships that have better-than-average performance.

Second, rollups typically had different investment objectives than the original partnerships. Where an original partnership specified cash-only investing and a defined liquidation period, it could be rolled up into a master security allowing leveraged investing and an infinite life structure. Thus, they were unfair to all investors who were forced into a security that differed substantially from the stated objectives of their original investment.

Another strategy typical of general partners masterminding rollups was to eliminate the subordination and incentive fee structures of the original partnerships. Instead of being compensated based on performance, they changed the formula to one which compensates them solely based on the size of the new assets under management, irrespective of whether it was meeting its stated investment objectives. Along the same lines, subtle changes in management fees often resulted in grossly increased compensation for the general partners.

But the most significant problem with rollups is that, in the real world of the securities market, investors experienced an immediate and substantial income loss and capital loss. In one typical rollup, the general partners promised a 10 percent yield based on a $15 per-share exchange value for the original partnership units. But in terms of the actual yield on the original investment, this amount really represented a decline from an 8.25 percent yield to a 6.5% yield. Moreover, to provide the $1.50 per-year yield, the rolled up entity actually would have had to dig into cash reserves to pay out the regular principal payments received from its mortgage-backed securities, so that the promised yield was in fact partially to a return *of* capital, as opposed to return *on* capital.

Further, after an exchange was made and the securities were traded with other REITs on the open market, the actual value of shares was typically but a fraction of the exchange value at which original partnership units were redeemed. In one notorious rollup, unhappy former limited partners found that shares they acquired for $30 each in exchange for their partnership units were trading for less than $6 per share on the very first day! (See Figure 5.4.)

It soon became evident that the effect of rollups was to devalue the original limited partnerships, and that they fundamentally threatened the existence of the secondary market for partnership units. No matter how carefully a partnership unit is evaluated, how much would you pay for it if it is likely to be rolled up and substantially devalued at some unknown date in the future?

Opposition to rollups has been tremendous. It was initially led by the dealers in the partnership resale market. They and other organizations including the American Association of Limited Partners, the International Association for Financial Planning, the National Center for Financial Education, the Consumer Federation of America and other groups launched a major public relations and lobbying effort that has largely stemmed the rollup tide. The SEC has promulgated new rules improving the ability of investors to fight rollups by requiring fuller disclosure on proxies and extending the review period. The NASD has put a stop to the biased compensation scheme for gathering proxies that paid brokers for "yes" votes but gave nothing for "no" votes. Further, investors have been put on alert, so it is no longer possible for general partners to attempt a rollup without arousing considerable investor resistance. Legislation that will permanently end the rollup problem is in progress. Unfair rollups are still a threat now, but, and with the passage of legislation, they should disappear completely. The legislation will allow fair rollups that truly benefit limited partners.

Quite a few issues remain unresolved in regulation of the partnership secondary market, and significant improvements need still to be made. As regulations continue to be fine-tuned to address the market's unique characteristics, investors on both the buy and sell side will be better served. Modifying current securities and tax laws to allow for the creation of a NASDAQ-

FIGURE 5.4   Real Estate Rollups Decimate Limited Partner Equity*

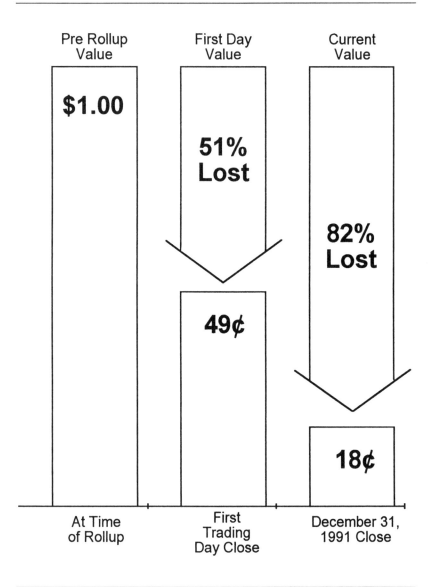

*Per $1 of investor exchange or equity value in all *Real Estate* rollups since 1983 per-proxy statement. Exchange value is appraised investor equity (assets less liabilities) at time of rollup.

SOURCE: Liquidity Fund "Rollup Performance" chart dated 12/31/91.

type display would encourage more firms to enter the market, improve trading and ultimately create a better pricing environment—all through the enhanced availability of information. Markups and spreads will decrease as trading volume expands and more interest develops in the lesser-known partnerships, creating better liquidity options for existing limited partners.

Our goal in highlighting these issues is to foster better understanding among investors, brokers, planners and regulatory agencies. As regulation of the partnership resale market is rationalized and standardized, the result will be to maximize liquidity and pricing efficiency for investors, and to make it easier for broker-dealer firms to meet their responsibilities to their customers.

CHAPTER 6

Controversies and Issues

The partnership resale market has earned its share of criticism, as happens to any human endeavor that threatens to change the status quo. As one might expect, many critics have legitimate complaints, while other criticisms stem from ignorance or long-standing but outmoded bias. Below we look at some of the key issues that have arisen during the growth of the secondary market. We attempt not only to show how controversies have emerged, but also to lend some perspective so that the reader can understand their context and form a balanced view of each issue.

DIRECT SOLICITATION

Some antipathy toward the partnership secondary market stems from accusations that certain firms have used abusive sales tactics to induce limited partners to sell their units. Taken to an extreme, proponents of this view insist that the secondary market for limited partnerships exists more as a result of such high-pressure sales tactics than from investors' own demands for liquidity.

Contacting limited partners directly by mail or telephone has been not only the most cost-efficient way to educate investors about the existence of the secondary market, but also a practical necessity because of the unique nature of the secondary market. Most limited partners are not aware that a secondary market exists for their units because disclaimers in limited partnerships' original offering materials have explicitly stated that no such market exists. Moreover, many general partners receiving inquiries from limited partners who wish to sell will direct them only to listing services sponsored by the general partners themselves or by the broker that underwrote the offering. Without direct solicitation, limited partners might never know an alternative exists.

Broker-dealers' net capital requirements further drive the need to contact potential unit sellers directly. The adverse impact on net capital created by trading limited partnerships—which under current SEC regulations are considered to have no value in calculating net capital requirements—constrains a dealer's ability to provide liquidity. Dealers who wish to maintain a continuous market must carefully manage their inventory and capital by limiting the size of their equity positions or by maintaining the positions for only a limited time. Because of the relatively small number of dealers and the restricted number of units they can hold at any given time, a continuous two-sided market can only be maintained by contacting individual limited partners when and as the need arises to secure a sufficient supply of units.

Through cold calls or direct mail, such efforts to contact limited partners do not in themselves constitute high-pressure sales techniques. For example, when an ethical dealer contacts limited partners, the gesture does not represent an overt offer to buy units. Rather, it is designed rather to inform limited partners that a secondary market exists for their units, to describe the reasons that may prompt an investor to consider liquidating, and to provide information about the dealer itself. A sample of a typical direct mail piece is shown in Figure 6.1. After contact is made, the ball lies in the limited partners' court. If they wish to sell, they now know what to do. Further, even if they solicit a bid for their units, they typically have up to several weeks to change their mind before the dealer's offer expires.

Of course, within any given industry, unscrupulous methods of doing business may exist. Therefore, it should not be surprising if high-pressure sales techniques occasionally crop up. These techniques, also referred to as "boiler room" tactics, have occurred in virtually every area of the securities business at one

FIGURE 6.1   Direct Mail Advertising for Sellers

LIQUIDITY FUND
INVESTMENT CORPORATION

February 28, 1991

RE: Sample Relp Name

Mr. John Q. Sample
Sample Title
Sample Company
1234 Sample Street
Samplecity, CA 99999

Dear Mr. Samples:

You can now get cash for your limited partnership units. Liquidity
Fund is the oldest and largest purchaser of limited partnerships.
Since 1980, we have purchased partnerships worth more than $150
million from over 17,000 limited partners. We are interested in
acquiring additional units in economically successful partnerships,
including one which public records indicate you own -- SAMPLE RELP
NAME.

You may wish to consider some of the following reasons why other
investors have sold to Liquidity Fund:

<u>Cash Now</u>
   * Receive a lump sum payment now, not smaller distributions
      over many years.
   * Don't hold the program for the remainder of its full life
      cycle.

<u>End Tax Complications & Costs</u>
   * Eliminate filing extensions due to K-1 delays and simplify
      the preparation of future tax returns.
   * Decrease tax preparation costs which may no longer be
      deductable.

<u>New Plans or Changed Expectations</u>
   * Investment objectives changed and they wanted to redirect
      their cash to a better-suited investment or to personal
      needs.
   * The partnership had not been living up to their original
      expectations or they were uncomfortable with the future
      outlook.

Call <u>1-(800)-833-3360</u> now to find out how much cash you can
receive for your partnership units. After you receive our offer, you
should review the partnership's current operating and financial
statements, plus your own circumstances, before making a decision to
sell.

Sincerely yours,

Sara Malone

Sara Malone
Acquisitions Vice President

TO RECEIVE A NO OBLIGATION OFFER, COMPLETE AND MAIL THIS COUPON OR CALL US AT
1-(800)-833-3360. LIST ANY OTHER PARTNERSHIPS YOU OWN AND INDICATE THE NUMBER
OF UNITS OF EACH. IF MORE SPACE IS NEEDED, PLEASE USE THE BACK OF THIS FORM.

                    PARTNERSHIP NAME: #UNITS:
Sample Relp Name _____ (ABCDE)) _____

_____ _____
_____ _____

Mr. John Q. Sample   PHONE (DAY): _____
Sample Title   PHONE (EVE): _____
Sample Company   (Please indicate proper
1234 Sample Street   phone number)
Samplecity, CA 99999
(Please correct if necessary)   0000000   AAAA11111

LIQUIDITY FUND INVESTMENT CORPORATION

FIGURE 6.1   Direct Mail Advertising for Sellers (continued)

You Can Sell Your Limited Partnership For Cash

Call us toll-free for a no-obligation price quotation.

LIQUIDITY FUND
INVESTMENT CORPORATION

For Public or Private Partnerships call:
1-800-833-3360

Liquidity Fund - The Recognized Leader

Forbes

"If you ever have to get out of a limited partnership, Brent Donaldson, (president of Liquidity Fund) may be the man you turn to. Donaldson looks for partnerships of some years standing that have built some actual equity for the investor."

Money

"The important thing is to know where to look for the highest price. Your best outlet, says tax expert Robert Stanger, editor of the Stanger Report, probably is Liquidity Fund Investment Corp. It regularly appraises real estate partnerships and offers to buy them."

FINANCIAL PLANNING
THE MAGAZINE FOR FINANCIAL SERVICE PROFESSIONALS

"Consider the plight of a doctor (who prefers to remain anonymous). In 1984, he invested $300,000, which he agreed to pay over six years, into a private real estate offering that was designed to generate $600,000 in tax deductions over the same period. Today, thanks to the 1986 tax act, his tax benefits are severely devalued, yet he still owes $150,000. Like many investors who bought into so-called real estate tax shelters, the doctor felt that he had the financial rug pulled out from under him. But his story, at least, has a happy ending. We took him out, says Bob Condon, a senior vice president at Liquidity Fund in Emeryville, California, the largest purchaser of partnership interests on the secondary market. We paid him $10,000 in cash and relieved him of all further liability on his investor note."

Liquidity Fund is an independent securities firm dealing in the secondary market for real estate limited partnerships. It is not affiliated with any investment product sponsor or securities firm.

We Are Currently Purchasing More Than 300 Public and Private Partnerships

The list is constantly being expanded

We review new partnerships every day. Please contact us about a free evaluation.

What partnerships will Liquidity Fund buy?

Liquidity Fund buys both public and private limited partnerships.

Over 17,000 investors have sold partnership units worth more than $150 million to Liquidity Fund since 1980.

LIQUIDITY FUND
INVESTMENT CORPORATION

1900 POWELL STREET, 7TH FLOOR
EMERYVILLE, CALIFORNIA 94608-1831

FIGURE 6.1 Direct Mail Advertising for Sellers (continued)

Over 17,000 Limited Partners Have Sold to Liquidity Fund and Cashed Out Early Since 1980

It's Easy To Work With Liquidity Fund

Liquidity Fund - The Recognized Leader

"... publicly registered limited partnerships are turning out to have some liquidity. So the advantages that such partnerships offer can now be augmented by the liquidity that has usually characterized other securities. As a result investors who need cash or are looking for a better return elsewhere are now finding it easier to sell their interests."

Contact Liquidity Fund for more information on the services we offer Limited Partners:

For Public or Private Partnerships call:

1-800-833-3360

You may also wish to consider selling now because:

1 You would rather receive a lump-sum cash payment now than a series of smaller payments over many years.

2 You do not want to wait for the completion of the typical partnership's ten to fifteen year total life.

3 Your financial planning needs have changed and you have a more suitable investment option.

4 You want to avoid the increased cost or complexity of filing more complicated tax returns due to tax reform.

◆ **Transfers are simple**

We take care of all the details. We have processed over 17,000 transactions in more than 400 different limited partnerships since 1980.

◆ **Transfers are safe**

Liquidity Fund is a member of the National Association of Securities Dealers (NASD) and securities are insured by the Security Investor Protection Corporation(SIPC).

◆ **Liquidity Fund evaluations are accurate**

In a study of 418 properties which were sold by partnerships over the last five years (total sales of approximately $4.0 billion), the average real property sales price we use to determine our values proved to be within 6% of the actual sales price achieved in the marketplace.

LIQUIDITY FUND
INVESTMENT CORPORATION
1900 POWELL STREET, 7TH FLOOR
EMERYVILLE, CALIFORNIA 94608-1831

The price Liquidity Fund offers may be more or less than the original cost of the interests. We can give no assurance that holding the interest for the duration of the partnership will be worth more or less than the price offered.

time or another. They could involve urging limited partners to sell by creating fear in their minds about the future performance of their investments. The caller may, for example, exaggerate or even fabricate negative aspects of the partnership's performance and suggest that the partnership could fail completely, and that the distribution might be reduced or eliminated. Although such sales practices may occur, they are certainly the exception rather than the rule. Such a sales pitch is indeed inherently illogical. Why would a broker want to buy a limited partner's interests if the partnership is truly doomed to failure?

Allegations that abusive sales tactics are common are often promoted by those who appear to have an economic interest in impeding the further development of the secondary market. Typically, they are general partners and sponsors (who fear that further market growth will impair their ability to raise capital for new issues) and industry organizations that represent them. Actually, a system of checks and balances operates within the partnership secondary market. If a given dealer developed a reputation for hounding limited partners to sell their units, the firm simply would not get very much repeat business from securities brokers to handle transactions on their behalf.

In fact, partnership dealers have a vested interest in maintaining high standards of professionalism and integrity. Their interest clearly lies in overall market growth and increasing the volume of trade. For such growth to occur, buyers, sellers, legislators and regulators must continue to observe that the key dealers are fairly and openly providing a legitimate service to the securities industry.

DEALER RESERVES

Problems can arise when a secondary market firm handling customer accounts does not have adequate procedures in place to ensure that customer capital and securities are protected. It is essential to maintain an adequate cushion of reserves for the customer's protection, but some firms fail to do so because increasing special contingency reserves represent a deduction from aggregate capital, and has an impact on the firm's net capital level. Rather than deplete their limited working capital, some firms, in fact, do not set aside any reserves at all.

Two types of special reserves are involved. The first simply represents the cash received from the unit purchaser, which is held in a "reserve" account until the units are actually delivered. Because the title transfer process involves so much paperwork, months can elapse before the units get officially registered in the buyer's name. Although the dealer may have already received advance payment for the units, there is always the possibility that something can go wrong and the transaction will fall through. Even if the transfer proceeds smoothly, the process occasionally can take as long as six months. So rather than putting buyer cash into working capital, the prudent firm will usually place it in an off-the-books trust account until the money is actually earned by delivering the units to the buyer.

The second type of reserve covers distributions due the buyer, but mistakenly sent to the seller. Some dealers guarantee that the buyer will receive partnership distributions as of a specified date. Because many general partners do not coordinate ownership transfers with partnership distributions, partnerships frequently send distributions to the original owner of the units even though the partnership may have been notified that a change of ownership has occurred. The dealer guaranteeing the distributions pays the new owner out of its own reserve account, then tracks down the seller to recover its out-of-pocket expense. The dealer carefully monitors announcements of distributions from the partnerships it trades, augmenting the reserve account as needed to cover the necessity of paying the distributions itself.

Because tracking distributions is an elaborate undertaking, many firms choose not to guarantee distributions. Some who do guarantee distributions may not maintain adequate reserves to cover them. The regulatory agencies have failed to keep a close enough watch on this aspect of back-office operations, possibly because of a lack of familiarity with the issues involved and the complexity of the recordkeeping process.

PRICING ISSUES

Without question, no topic of discussion involving the secondary market has caused more controversy than pricing issues. While critics of the market may oversimplify matters by labeling dealers as "vultures" taking unfair advantage of partnership owners who wish to sell, pricing issues are truly complex and merit closer examination. Essentially, there are three distinct calculations that, combined, determine the ultimate price paid for partnership units: discounts, break-up values and markups.

Discounts

Unquestionably, dealers (based on their perception of buyer interest) buy at a discount from net asset value. It simply would make no economic or investment sense to pay $100 in cash today for something that *might* be worth $100 after a long wait. People who do not fully grasp the investment risk, research expense, and long waiting period for eventual benefits that are involved in purchasing partnership units might initially react negatively to this necessary discount, but once they put themselves in the shoes of the buyer, it becomes easy to understand.

In making a hard cash offer to buy partnership units, dealers are only willing to buy at a discount from break-up value that allows for analysis and evaluation expenses, the capital cost of maintaining inventory, extraordinary paperwork costs, risks inherent to partnership ownership, and a margin of profit upon resale.

Discounts from net asset values are a reality of free-market securities trading. Time and again throughout the eighties we witnessed corporate takeovers and buyouts where the buying side offered more than the current market price of a company's stock. Why? The underlying assets, if sold, were worth quite a bit more than the securities' trading price on the open market. In a liquid market where securities are instantly convertible to cash, the stocks of our largest corporations virtually always trade for less than the net value of the company's underlying assets—tangible and intangible. Such companies are sometimes taken over by savvy investors offering *more* than the trading price because they know that they can break up the company and sell the assets for an *even greater* amount.

Limited partnership interests are no different. The price sellers pay for liquidity is a discount that makes buyers feel they are getting a good value for their cash. Some form of discount is fundamental to the nature of the market, so the real issue here is the size of discount. We believe it will be possible for discounts to lessen, particularly if general partners increase their understanding of the market and join with dealers to bring about industry and regulatory changes that will benefit all parties.

One can argue about the size of A discount, but the discount itself is a fact of life. In the future, we expect discounts to move closer to net asset value as trading volume increases and as general partners adjust their practices to the growing resale market.

Break-Up Values

Naturally, some limited partners are disappointed when they receive a current valuation of their partnership units. Imagine, for example, a limited partner who for years has received partnership statements showing his original $1,000-per-unit investment, depreciation and income he has received, and an accounting calculation for the book value of his partnership assets, but who has never seen a true evaluation of current value. He observes that in the years since he originally invested, even though real estate performance has not been spectacular, housing prices in his community have gone up some, so he imagines that his investment has probably gone up some, too. He needs cash, and figures to at least get his original investment back, so he has his partnership units evaluated by a dealer.

They analyze his partnership, comprised of modestly leveraged retail, residential and office properties, and determine that the break-up value of the partnership unit —if the properties were to be sold today under current local market conditions—is $600 per unit. Because the partnership is leveraged, which means greater risk and less cash flow, and because the properties are located in troubled markets with no clear recovery in sight, the dealer calculates that a prudent discount is 40 percent from current break-up value. They offer him $360 per unit.

Imagine you are the general partner when this investor (or his broker or planner) calls you up, outraged. "I paid $1,000 per unit for this partnership, and they're saying it's only worth only $360! What happened to the rest of my investment!?" You are not likely to defend the pricing practices of the dealer. You are going to say something like, "Those vultures! They're always trying to gouge investors! Of course your investment is worth far more than what they are offering, since we are well-positioned to weather this downturn and come out well for our investors." And of course it is "worth" more than $360. It is worth $600 if all the assets were sold today, and maybe a lot more if markets turn around in a couple of years. But it's only liquidatable at $360 today because the assets *are not* being sold today, and whoever buys them will have to wait some time to realize their value.

The point is, general partners and brokers who originally sold units to limited partners have a far different perspective on secondary market valuation than do dealers. Dealer valuations are based on *today's* market conditions, not what the general partner believes the properties will be worth in the future. Their discounts place partnership interests on the same playing field as other potential uses for investment capital. Thus, dealers cast the hard light of reality on partnerships that, for years, may never have been carefully scrutinized by outside observers. In fact, many well-managed partnerships experienced devaluation during the eighties because of soft real estate conditions in key markets. As long as general partners do not sell properties, actual worth under adverse local market conditions is not a calculation they have any incentive to make or publicize. Their interest lies in maintaining the good faith of their limited partners while they ride through choppy economic seas towards better times ahead.

Dealers, on the other hand, have quite different interests. They must look carefully and closely at today's market values, at potential risk and at comparable investments. Naturally, dealers' partnership valuations differ from the general partners own valuations. They frequently have had the unfortunate role of being messengers with bad news. The message at times is that the original investment has not—to date—performed well. As unwelcome as such tidings may be to the seller or general partner, there is no need to shoot the messenger. Sellers are not under any obligation to sell. They can always hold onto their assets and look for a better offer, and since there are several dealer firms, it is advisable to do so.

Markups

When a broker-dealer purchases a security on behalf of a client and immediately resells it to the client, the difference between the broker's buying and selling prices is termed a "markup." All of the broker-dealer's expenses, plus its profit, must come out of this markup.

As a rule, markups in the partnership secondary market are high compared to markups prevalent in the secondary market for over-the-counter stocks. For this reason, markup practices have received some criticism. The NASD has confirmed in a recent release that its markup guidelines apply to these securities. It appears that in most circumstances 6 percent to 8 percent compensation is the norm for each side of a partnership secondary transaction. As we pointed out in some detail in Chapter 5 (see pp. 104), fundamental differences between the efficiency and ease of trading OTC stocks and the prolonged process of transferring ownership of partnership interests make OTC compensation norms inapplicable to the partnership secondary market. Further, until partnership unit transfer procedures are standardized it will be difficult to reduce the current norm in the partnership aftermarket. However, we look forward to increasing standardization, which may allow markups to become lower and more consistent with other areas of the securities business.

CHAPTER 7

The Future of the Secondary Market

What is destined for the secondary market over the coming years? One easy prediction is that it will change. We believe that key areas of change will include overall market growth, better dissemination of information, regulatory and legislative refinements and industry standardization.

MARKET GROWTH: THE NEXT FIVE YEARS

People familiar with the primary partnership market—new issue partnerships which are the source of the units later available on the secondary market—note that the dollar volume of new issues has declined from a peak of more than $18 billion in 1984 to some $4 billion in 1990. If new issues are in such a decline, won't the secondary market also get smaller?

The answer is not as simple as it might seem because many factors come into play. Analyzing all the variables that will affect the size of the market, our best estimate is that it will continue to increase at its current rate of 15 percent to 20 percent over the next five years. After that, the market will either stabilize, maintaining a relatively constant volume of trade, or it will continue to grow at a much slower rate for another 5 to 10 years, declining thereafter.

The Partnership Cycle and Trading Volume

The secondary market is most active in public partnerships that are at least 5 years old, and oftentimes 10 to 15 years old. The life cycle of a partnership has been typically at least 15 years, and more recently seems to be extending to 20 years and more. This means that the universe of partnerships typically traded in the secondary market includes all public partnerships issued from 5 years ago to 15 or 20 years ago. The number of public partnerships issued 15 to 20 years ago that may complete their life cycle over the next five years is small—probably less than $4 billion worth—compared to the $40 billion of public partnerships issued in 1986 through 1990 that will be added over the next five years to the active secondary market trading universe. Thus, the market will grow because more mature partnerships will be coming into it than will be leaving it. (See Figure 7.1.)

Increase in Trading Activity

An absolute increase in the amount of partnership interests qualified for trading in the secondary market is just one element that makes us confident of our 15 percent to 20 percent annual growth prediction. In any given year, less than 1 percent of the units of qualifying partnerships are traded, usually the range is .5 percent to .75 percent. Inevitably, as the market is better known, more and more holders of partnership units will realize that they have a liquidity option, and more limited partners will choose to exercise it. Imagine that as small a number as 1.5 percent decide to sell next year. The market would double in size from this year. A much smaller increase in the number of people deciding to sell—from three-quarters of 1 percent to nine-tenths of 1 percent—would cause this market to grow by 20 percent.

Rising Prices Produce More Sellers

For a number of reasons we outline below (see "Pricing"), we believe that trading values will rise closer to portfolio values. If this proves true, the seller who decided not to sell at a low price a year ago will be able sell at a higher price, and trading volume

FIGURE 7.1   New Partnership Sales and Secondary Market Trading Volume

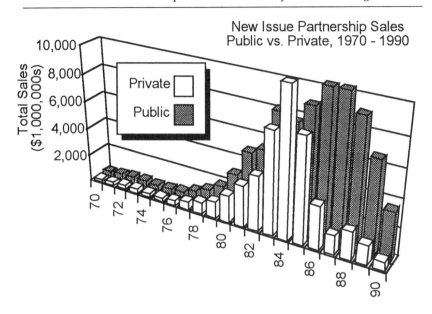

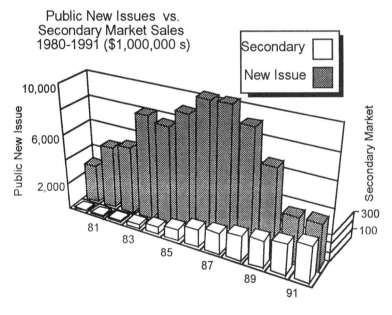

SOURCE: Robert A. Stanger & Co., Shrewsbury, New Jersey.

will increase. Moreover, as values rise, the dollar transaction volume for any particular partnership increases, even if the number of sellers remains stable. Third, as the value of the partnerships rise, a greater percentage of investors overall will want to cash out to take advantage of higher prices. So we believe that the general trend of rising prices will also stimulate market growth.

Increase in the Percentage of Qualifying Partnerships

Consider the number of partnerships that currently are not doing well. Right now, less than 20 percent of the $90 billion in publicly registered partnerships issued through 1985 are surviving and thriving enough to create possible secondary market interest. Yet, to date, only 5 percent or so of such partnerships are actively traded because only those have sufficient performance to justify reasonable buyer interest. As more of the 20 percent stabilize their asset operations with the help of economic recovery and —in the case of real estate partnerships—a decrease in vacancy rates, they will begin to capture the interest of secondary market investors.

These partnerships have pent-up seller demand—a small percentage of unit holders who previously would have liquidated their interests if they had been able to, and who now will be able to sell for the first time. Clearly, economic recovery will bring an extra influx of sellers to the market. If the percentage of qualifying partnerships increases merely 5 percent, that in itself will enlarge the secondary market universe by 25 percent.

Thus, a number of trends—improving economics within the partnerships themselves, pricing moving closer to portfolio values, increased availability of information about the market, and an absolute increase in the size of the universe of tradable partnerships—all point to the same direction. Looking at how these factors reinforce each other, we foresee a strong growth trend—in the range of 15 percent to 20 percent per year—that will double the size of the market within five years. Further, if several of these trends combine more forcefully or earlier than expected, the growth rate could be even higher (40 percent to 50 percent) in a given year.

MARKET CONTINUES FOR 20 YEARS

We find it difficult to make predictions of market size more than five years hence because we have no way of knowing the volume of limited partnership interests to be issued in the next few years. The volume of new issues over the next five years is a key factor in determining what the size of the secondary market will be ten to fifteen years from now.

Certainly in the first two years of this decade the new issue market is quite low compared to the mid-eighties, but we will see what happens later. REITS made something of a comeback after basically dropping off the face of the earth in the mid-seventies. So it is not outside the realm of possibility that partnerships will enjoy something of a comeback, probably falling well short of the volume in their heyday, but sparking enough interest to merit an active secondary market.

We do know, however, that a tremendous amount of capital went into partnership interests between 1981 and 1991. If it is at least 15 years from the date of issuance until the date of liquidation, and 20 years in most cases, the lives of these partnerships will extend to the years 2000 through as late as 2010. So we can say that a solidly viable market for secondary interests will exist for at least for another 15 to 20 years.

PRICING

Currently, discounts from break-up value in many cases are substantial. While discounts will never disappear, they will get smaller, and units will trade at prices closer to actual portfolio values. Several key factors keep dealer discounts substantial:

- Heavy research and analysis costs are spread over a relatively small volume of trade.
- Portfolio information is difficult to obtain, which increases research and analysis costs.
- Transferring ownership of units is quite costly because of the lack of standardization of transfer procedures.

- Obtaining current, accurate bid and ask pricing is problematic without a centralized information exchange system
- Capital costs are high because of current SEC net capital regulations.
- State blue-sky regulations are haphazard, out of date and lack standardization, which limits trading in many states.

We have little doubt that trading volume will increase steadily. As volume increases, pricing will improve. Other factors may take some time to change, but it is truly in the interest of all parties—buyers, sellers, general partners, dealers, brokers/planners and regulators—to standardize the industry, better publicize portfolio values, centralize trading information and rationalize capital requirements and other regulations. Much progress has been made in the regulatory discussion, and we expect that at the NASD and SEC level, emerging guidelines and rulings will help the market considerably. As all these changes occur, the cost of analyzing and transfering ownership will be reduced further and further, bringing pricing ever closer to net asset value.

Another key factor with respect to pricing is the general perception of limited partnerships on the part of investors. Investors may like real estate, oil and gas, cable TV or equipment leasing, but if partnerships are perceived as bad because of rollups or other abuses by general partners, then secondary market prices are mediocre. If general partners are able to prove over time that they can perform well for investors, pricing will improve because of increased consumer confidence.

MARKET SEGMENTS

Our predictions of overall market growth are based in large part on analysis of the real estate segment of the secondary market. On a dollar volume basis, real estate represents about half of the $132 billion in total public and privately placed partnerships issued since 1970, and more than half of all transactions in the secondary market. The same growth trends will affect other segments—oil and gas, equipment leasing, cable TV and miscellaneous other segments—but future growth in these areas is harder to predict because evolving technology and world markets may have a far greater positive or negative impact on these investments. Below we identify key factors that will play a role in determining each segment's growth.

Equipment Leasing

Financially, virtually all equipment leasing partnerships are structured similarly, but the underlying assets are varied. For any equipment partnership, the key questions are, "What will demand be for the equipment being leased?" "How long will demand last?" and "What will the residual value be when the lease expires?" Special circumstances affect each type of equipment. For airplanes, not only do we have an unstable airline industry, but new regulations may require refitting engines to be quieter and more fuel-efficient, which might hurt the residual value of nonrefitted aircraft. Further, there is increasing demand for airlines to rid themselves of older planes because of concerns about metal fatigue. This could cause a glut of less desired equipment. Containers are subject to the worldwide supply of shipping containers. Railroad cars have more predictable demand. Computers may have little or no residual value.

Nonetheless, in recent years the equipment lease has been exciting to investors because of the high current return, despite the unpredictability of future demand for various types of equipment. In terms of total capital invested, new-issue equipment leasing partnerships outpaced oil and gas for the first time in 1987 and drew close to real estate in 1990. Thus, a lot of equipment leasing partnerships with high cash flow will be available to the secondary market over the next five years. Consequently, secondary market trading in this area will increase substantially, but it is difficult to pin a number on trading growth because of variables external to the secondary market. These external variables, taken together, translate into risk as to what the residual value will be, and residual value is crucial in determining the total return on investment as a partnership nears the end of leasing periods and begins liquidating assets.

Oil and Gas

Energy programs have fallen off in popularity since the downturn in energy prices in the early eighties. However, new-issue oil and gas partnerships have continued to come out in a steady, if smaller, stream, and plenty of viable energy programs will come onto the secondary market. Their prospects are solely dependent on the price of oil and gas.

Despite the fall-off in the rate of new issues, more than $16 billion in public oil and gas programs came out from 1979 through 1990. Either a rise or a drop in oil prices could cause a flurry of trading activity, but otherwise, this will be a slower area of secondary market growth.

Cable TV

Cable partnerships are under clouds of potential regulation and technological innovation. Even though they have done spectacularly to date, many secondary market investors are shying away or holding back from them.

The regulatory cloud is a controversy as to whether cable monopolies in local markets, granted to provide incentive for installing cable systems, should or should not be maintained. If not maintained, some believe that increased competition could erode cable operating margins. Others maintain that even with the loss of monopolies, serious competition is unlikely because the cost of installing infrastructure is high, so existing systems will maintain attractive pricing.

The concept of stand-alone satellite reception in each home, effectively bypassing cable systems, is the technological cloud deterring some investors. But even though such technology is conceivable, the installed base is so many years away that there will be no immediate effect on performance of cable partnerships. In the meantime, cable seems to have tremendous opportunity to increase revenues dramatically with its existing installed base through pay-per-view programming for sporting and cultural events. "Addressability" or the technology which lets you call to your home any movie from the Turner library, for example, while your neighbor chooses another movie (or the same movie a half hour later) is another potential source of revenue. However, it is probably too far down the line to consider in evaluating partnerships. In any case, with only some $2 billion of cable public partnerships issued, this segment will not be a big factor in overall secondary market growth.

MARKET PLAYERS

Currently the secondary market is segmented, with independent dealer firms comprising one area of trading activity. While the major NYSE wirehouses internal systems are currently closed, it is worthwhile pointing out that transactions between buyers and sellers of interests in partnerships originally issued by the wirehouse will in the future not be at prices divergent from the rest of the market. Pricing in these two segments was not closely related formerly, and the segregation of these two market areas is truly a disadvantage to both buyers and sellers as a new format emerges it appears that one market price will exist.

Other players in the market include smaller broker-dealers, general partners and independent exchange services.

Independent Dealers

Right now, independent secondary market firms not affiliated with other brokerage operations, or those set up as a segregated subsidiary of a brokerage firm, comprise about 50 percent of the market volume. A few of these firms, in business for eight or ten years, have substantial capitalization and solid customer bases. In addition, there are a number of smaller firms that have entered the market in the last few years. Increased regulatory pressures may cause some of these recent arrivals to have difficulties in the market. Over the next five years or so, the handful of well-capitalized secondary market firms that have established standardized practices will survive, thrive and provide increased services in this market.

Major "Wirehouse" Firms

Major brokerage firms, such as Merrill Lynch and PaineWebber comprise the remaining 50 percent of the market. They do a tremendous amount of volume, but you see little publicity about them. They have two reasons for not having publicized the secondary market: One, when initial issue sales were thriving, the secondary market would have competed for investment capital with their new issues; and two, prices in the secondary market often are lower than what was originally invested. The wirehouses are not eager to advertise to their clients the difficulties these investments have been having.

Those firms formerly provided buyer-seller matching services, even if they weren't publicizing them. They have a small number of buyers and and a large number of sellers. Going forward, wirehouses will likely begin to use services of outside secondary market firms to purchase when they don't have buyers, or to sell when they don't have sellers.

This is because major wirehouses, interestingly, even if they are able to act as matchmakers, they won't be able to act as a dealer with inventory. If somebody wants to sell, they will likely be forced to go to the secondary market firms if there is no internal buyer. That's because they are precluded by law from acting as a dealer and putting their own firm's capital into a security of which they were also the issuer. So some involvement from secondary market firms will be required as the wirehouse segment of the market starts coming in line with regulations that affect trading of all securities.

Once there is increased clarification as to how the secondary market regulations will be imposed, wirehouses will have increased comfort about working with secondary market firms. Over time, the increasing track record and growth of the stronger secondary market firms will also help them understand that the secondary market business is not a pariah, but provides good and valuable services to investors who want to get in or out. Additionally, wirehouses are engaged in no competitive new-issue business to speak of, so the secondary market is not as threatening to their new product sales as it once was perceived, validly or not. Certainly these firms will have increasing numbers of clients who want to sell over time, and from the perspective of providing service to clients, they will increase their interest in and involvement with dealer firms to help find buyers. It is easier for them to help people get out rather than to set up roadblocks.

Smaller Broker-Dealers

A few smaller broker-dealers currently use secondary market firms to sell or buy interests, while many as yet do nothing in the market. Broker-dealers who are not actively involved as dealers, and who are not major wirehouses with a lot of proprietary products, increasingly will find themselves acting as agents or riskless principals for investors who want to get in or out. There will be a lot more activity from many additional firms not currently active in the market.

General Partners

General partners will face increasing pressure to standardize their documents and provide additional disclosure in financial reports as to the performance of underlying assets on an asset-by-asset basis, as opposed to a consolidated basis. And, abusive general partner rollups will, it is hoped, cease to exist. Right now it appears that rollups have dwindled to almost nil because of the terrible publicity and the proposed legislation in Congress that have come in response to rollup abuses. To the extent that unfair rollups cease, pricing will increase in the secondary market. The many potential buyers who are afraid to invest because of the prospect of being caught up in a rollup will come back into the market.

Exchanges

An existing auction exchange, known as the National Partnership Exchange (NAPEX), has played a small role thus far. Its future depends on its own ability to manage and promote a business, and whether it can hammer out a larger role for itself. Most secondary market firms find they are able to do their business much more efficiently without using a third-party exchange service.

NAPEX is a matching firm that also tries to provide all the paperwork and settlement as well. There lies the key complication. Most secondary market firms and the brokers who deal with them prefer to allow the settlement and transfer process to be carried out by one of the secondary market firms rather than handing it off to a third party, where control is lost. Without standardization and regular-way settlement, the ability to provide better settlement services is an area in which all the secondary market firms are very competitive, and is a key service they use to distinguish themselves from each other.

This fact is a huge impediment to the success of the concept of an independent exchange/transfer agency. A simpler and more likely exchange is the NASD activating an electronic bulletin board listing bid and asking prices (see below), and simply letting dealers contact each other and effect their own transfers. Functionally, this is what happens on most securities exchanges. An exchange run by the NASD would be more efficient, better regulated and have higher broker-dealer confidence than a service operated by an independent player.

STANDARDIZATION

Some of the more forward-thinking general partners have already begun to do things to improve the value of limited partner's holdings on the secondary market: making ex-dividend policies clearer and transfers more frequent; standardizing and shortening transfer documentation; providing for Section 754 elections; and increasing disclosure of asset-by-asset financial information. Further standardization of the general partners' practices will come in part voluntarily, and in part because the SEC and the NASD will begin to impose standardization over time. As general partners come more fully into the real world of the securities business, using transfer agents and not acting as islands unto themselves, they will start interacting with people more sophisticated in the exigencies of securities trades who can help set up operations that more closely parallel those of other securities. As a result, partnership interests will become more readily tradable.

Standardizing the back office takes time, energy and money, so some general partners will be slow to get on board. Change will come not only from the demands of increased secondary market activity, but also from greater regulatory clarity from the SEC, NASD and IRS. An NASD committee has been working for nearly two years on the secondary market regulation and standardization, determining how rules and guidelines pertaining to equities and fixed-income investments should apply to partnerships. As we write this book in early 1992, we expect by sometime in 1993 a series of comprehensive and far-reaching reports, clarifications and technical arrangements will come out that will give notice to NASD member firms about how various aspects of the market should and will work.

Such clarification will help to minimize differences in practices between various secondary firms and wirehouse matching services, and will provide standard direction to the general partners and the broker-dealers who act as agents on behalf of sellers and buyers.

NASD ELECTRONIC BULLETIN BOARD

We expect that the NASD may request the IRS to rule on whether an electronic bulletin board listing service will be allowed without triggering the adverse tax consequences of treating partnerships as publicly traded corporations. Under the safe harbor rules for publicly traded partnerships, it seems that a secondary market bulletin board should not cause a problem as long as not more than 5 percent of the partnership trades hands in any given year. If the IRS rules favorably, it is highly likely that partnerships will be listed on the NASD OTC electronic bulletin board. That would be a great leap forward in standard information dissemination. It would increase trade volume and price efficiencies, bringing trading prices closer to break-up values.

A number of secondary market firms are firm, vocal proponents of activating such a centralized electronic listing system. This flies in the face of the accusation that secondary market firms thrive on inefficiencies because such a listing service would significantly increase efficiency. These firms believe a listing service would also increase volume by accelerating standardization and reducing many of the extraordinary costs that currently necessitate such a difference between the bid and asking price.

Ultimately, such an electronic listing service, because of the increased standardization and efficiency it entails, would increase prices to sellers, which would benefit everybody involved. Sellers, of course, would receive more cash for their units. General partners would benefit because their limited partners would achieve better value for their investments. Buyers would benefit because more of their investment dollar would go into assets, and less into transaction costs. Brokers and planners acting as agents would find it easier to serve their clients. And dealers would have lower transaction costs and increased volume.

Thus, a centralized electronic listing service would truly be a watershed event in terms of the future of the market. After it is instituted, we think there will be a lot more sell interest on the part of limited partners, an increased willingness on the part of brokers to make buy or sell recommendations to investors, and, overall, greatly enhanced liquidity for limited partnership investors.

CHAPTER 8

A Plan for Better Cooperation Between Dealers and General Partners

That partnership units trade at a discount to real portfolio values is a given. However, the view that dealers are solely responsible for the large discounts prevalent in the secondary market, and that they are trying to keep prices down, is fundamentally misguided. What many people do not realize is the extent to which general partners, not dealers, are responsible for the relatively low valuation of partnership units in the secondary market. We believe trading prices could increase between 20 percent and 50 percent if a number of steps, some quite simple, were put into practice by general partners. As a start, we cite four suggestions put forth by Robert Stanger in his opinion article in the May 1991 issue of *Stanger's Investment Advisor:*

General partners can improve market prices by supporting (rather than fighting) the secondary market in the following ways:

1. Support Market Makers and Analysts. General partners should seek to establish relationships with reputable analysts and market makers, keeping them abreast of partnership events and financial conditions. The "regular" stock market works the same way. Financial PR is not bad. The purpose is very legitimate—to ensure partnership securities are adequately understood and supported in the market.

2. Make Asset Performance Information Available. General partners should disclose more detailed portfolio performance information, including portfolio values. General partners must know values to manage portfolios well. It's high time such estimates of value, properly hedged to keep the lawyers happy, are made available to buyers, sellers, dealers and holders of limited partnership interests . . . .

3. Eliminate the Potential Tax Traps in Secondary Market Purchases. General partners can make an accounting adjustment on the partnership's books (a so-called Section 754 election) that enables a unit buyer to avoid assuming the low tax basis of the selling partner . . . . Without the Section 754 election, the buyer's bid price for units is always reduced . . . to offset the future tax obligation. The election isn't without administrative cost, but perhaps it's time to consider the needs of departing limiteds as well as remaining limiteds.

4. Standardize Back Office Procedures. General partners could greatly lower transfer costs typically charged to the partnership by standardization. The result would also be to narrow pricing spreads and reduce discounts in the aftermarket . . . [S]tandardized transfer forms . . . and one set of transfer requirements . . . would reduce the cost of the transfer to the buyer and seller (as well as to the partnership itself) and improve buyer and seller confidence in the process by allowing transfers to occur more rapidly.

Standardization is also needed in creating ex-dividend policies. In some cases, the dividend is sent to the person of record as of the last day of the month or quarter, but transfers aren't booked until the first day of the following month or quarter, [creating] a situation in which almost every transfer has to be negotiated differently, a process that is extremely labor-intensive and costly to track. The current dividend collecting headache definitely forces down secondary market pricing.

We fully endorse Mr. Stanger's four suggested changes in general partner practices, and propose four additional changes that we believe complete the picture. If all these changes are implemented, discounts and markups will lessen substantially, bringing trading prices much closer to actual portfolio values.

1. **Encourage an independent price dissemination system.** This would vastly improve market information, enabling buyers and sellers to obtain the best prices. NASD rules will require submittal of last trade pricing from all dealers (including NYSE firms); it should be encouraged to disseminate that data electronically to brokers.
2. **Distribute financial information more widely.** This is the easiest (and least expensive) thing general partners could do to increase buy interest. Services exist that distribute financial and performance information to thousands of brokerage offices, analysts, libraries, etc., for a relatively small annual per-partnership charge.
3. **Educate their limited partners.** Providing limited partners with information about the secondary market by explaining how it works and how to secure the best price will force all dealers to be more efficient.
4. **Pledge against rollups.** This will encourage brokers and their clients to enter the marketplace. Many do not invest because they fear rollups. Pricing would improve immediately if sponsors committed to no rollups on existing partnerships.

We believe that, taken together, these eight suggestions offer a rational guideline for cooperation between general partners and dealers that will benefit both parties, and will most certainly offer tremendous benefit to investors. Ten years ago the secondary market did not exist; today it is a well-established reality. The emergence of the secondary market may have been painful for some general partners whose poor performance was put into a spotlight, and certainly many involved in the business of issuing new partnerships perceived the secondary market as competition for investor capital.

Nonetheless, we believe the secondary market is a long-term benefit to the partnership industry for a number of reasons. It is a primary catalyst bringing industry standardization of valuation, pricing and financial reporting practices. The secondary market is stimulating federal, state and industry regulatory agencies to re-examine, update and standardize policies and guidelines related to partnership securities. Most importantly, by providing liquidity, the secondary market not only provides immediate benefits to current limited partners, it removes one of the greatest disincentives to investing in original-issue partnerships.

Ironically, the secondary market is experiencing a growth spurt during a period when the primary issue partnership market is having difficulty raising capital. Certainly many enlightened general partners already see that the secondary market can be a valuable ally to the primary market. Over time, we believe that this perception will become more widespread, and that increased cooperation between general partners, secondary market firms and regulatory agencies will develop. The end result, which we hope will evolve over the next very few years, will be a more open and better understood investment arena that attracts more capital to both the primary and secondary markets.

Appendixes

APPENDIX A

Limited Partnership Market Statistics

Public/Private Partnership Sales Totals*
(in Billions)

	Public Partnership Sales	Private Partnership Sales	Total Partnership Sales
Real Estate	45,276	23,720	68,996
Oil and Gas	20,188	12,040	32,228
Equipment Leasing	6,646	568	7,214
Cable TV	1,892	11,089	12,981
Miscellaneous	10,486	47,417	57,903
	84,488	94,834	179,322

*Totals are from 1970 through November 1990.

SOURCE: Robert A. Stanger & Co., Shrewsbury, New Jersey.

List of Firms Participating in the Secondary Market

Bigelow Management, Inc.
11 E. 44th Street, Suite 1100
New York, NY 10017
Contact: Glen Bigelow

Phone: (212) 697-5880
(800) 431-7811

Chicago Partnership Board
185 N. Wabash Avenue, Suite 1900
Chicago, IL 60601
Contact: Jim Frith

Phone: (312) 332-4100
(800) 272-6273

Cuyler & Associates
349 W. Commercial Street, Suite 1445
P.O. Box 619
E. Rochester, NY 14445
Contact: Virginia Cuyler

Phone: (800) 274-9991
(716) 586-9991

Dean Witter Reynolds
2 World Trade Center, 64th Floor
New York, NY 10048
Contact: Lynne Dierlam

Phone: (212) 392-8085

Equity Line Properties
9200 S. Dadeland Blvd., Suite 609
Miami, FL 33156
Contact: Bob Spielman   Phone: (305) 662-4088
                                               (800) 327-9990

Fox & Henry
6428 Dullet Road
Countryside, IL 60525
Contact: Marge Polaski   Phone: (708) 352-8710

Frain Asset Management
416 N. Bath Club Blvd.
N. Redington Beach, FL 33708
Contact: Paul Frain   Phone: (800) 654-6110

Liquidity Fund
1900 Powell Street, 7th Floor
Emeryville, CA 94608
Contact: Acquisitions Dept.   Phone: (510) 652-1462

MacKenzie Patterson
3685 Mt. Diablo Blvd., Suite 150
Lafayette, CA 94549
Contact: Pat Patterson   Phone: (415) 283-2263
         Bob Condon   (800) 854-8357

Merrill Lynch
World Financial Center–South Tower
New York, NY 10080-6104
Contact: Mike Morganbesser   Phone: (212) 236-5050

National Partnership Exchange
P.O. Box 578
Tampa, FL 33601-0578
Contact: Chris Tully   Phone: (813) 222-0555
                                               (800) 356-2739

National Partnership Marketplace
100 Galli Drive, Suite 8
Bel Marin Keys, CA 94949
Contact: Laura Lacey

Phone: (415) 456-8825
(415) 382-3555

Pacific Asset Group, Inc.
215 N. Marengo, Suite 115
Pasadena, CA 91101
Contact: Dan Breen

Phone: (818) 796-6693
(800) 727-7244

PaineWebber
1200 Harbor Blvd., 4th Floor
Weehawken, NJ 07087
Contact: Jennifer Chrystal

Phone: (201) 902-3101

Partnership Securities Exchange
1999 Harrison Street, Suite 720
Oakland, CA 94612
Contact: Jim Fotenos

Phone: (415) 763-5555
(800) 736-9797

Pre-Owned Partnerships
P.O. Box 1909
Annapolis, MD 21404
Contact: Brad Davidson

Phone: (800) 426-6656

Prudential Securities
199 Water Street, 33rd Floor
New York, NY 10805
Contact: John Sullivan

Phone: (212) 214-1000

Raymond James & Associates
880 Carillon Parkway
P.O. Box 12749
St. Petersburg, FL 33733
Contact: Dav. Mosby

Phone: (800) 248-8863
Extension 5055

Shearson Lehman Hutton
388 Greenwich Street, 37th Floor
New York, NY 10013
Contact: Michelle Magino   Phone: (212) 464-8647

Smith Barney
1345 Avenue of the Americas, 46th Floor
New York, NY 10105
Contact: Stacy Miller   Phone: (212) 698-5915

Springhill Financial Services
621 Palm Drive
Glendale, CA 91202
Contact: Larry Hales   Phone: (818) 507-0975
                                                  (800) 255-3264

Number of Limited Partners by State

PARTNERSHIP ROLLUPS ARE NOT A SMALL ISSUE!

Abusive limited partnership rollups are not an insignificant issue that may affect only a few voters. Rather, thousands of real people in each state/congressional district are affected by the potential abuses.

LIMITED PARTNERS BY STATE*

State	Number of Limited Partners	Average Investment
ALASKA	26,790	$ 9,556
ALABAMA	46,810	$11,096
ARKANSAS	24,300	$11,315
ARIZONA	130,210	$11,311
CALIFORNIA	1,541,910	$10,285
COLORADO	317,730	$ 7,723
CONNECTICUT	152,360	$11,073
WASH., D.C.	35,550	$12,300
DELAWARE	102,860	$ 5,952
FLORIDA	447,920	$12,322

*This data is derived from a computer analysis of the Liquidity Fund mailing lists of nearly 800,000 limited partners, approximately 10 percent of the total number of limited partners across the United States. We sorted our list geographically to determine the number of limited partners in each state. We then extrapolated each state's total by multiplying the count of limited partners on our list by a factor of 10 (since our list is 1/10 of the nationwide total).

State	Number of Limited Partners	Average Investment
GEORGIA	89,500	$11,836
HAWAII	44,690	$10,066
IOWA	77,260	$ 9,533
IDAHO	22,560	$10,007
ILLINOIS	321,520	$12,080
INDIANA	95,050	$11,165
KANSAS	83,620	$ 9,688
KENTUCKY	40,760	$11,916
LOUISIANA	48,630	$11,816
MASS.	273,750	$ 9,708
MARYLAND	151,770	$10,422
MAINE	18,320	$10,098
MICHIGAN	317,270	$10,119
MINNESOTA	233,650	$ 8,601
MISSOURI	163,030	$10,891
MISSISSIPPI	14,340	$10,091
MONTANA	32,210	$ 8,415
N. CAROLINA	116,520	$12,268
N. DAKOTA	13,830	$ 9,735
NEBRASKA	55,540	$10,211
NEW HAMP.	37,240	$10,477
NEW JERSEY	232,320	$11,300
NEW MEXICO	50,400	$ 9,825
NEVADA	25,040	$11,415
NEW YORK	749,750	$ 8,387
OHIO	260,630	$11,404
OKLAHOMA	44,250	$11,309
OREGON	99,250	$ 9,650
PENN.	253,940	$11,287
RHODE IS.	26,260	$10,525
S. CAROLINA	46,640	$11,417
S. DAKOTA	23,410	$ 9,772
TENNESSEE	73,000	$10,801
TEXAS	327,440	$11,145
UTAH	43,280	$ 9,648
VIRGINIA	197,060	$ 9,865
VERMONT	20,830	$12,026
WASHINGTON	229,250	$ 8,855
WISCONSIN	131,150	$ 9,580
W. VIRGINIA	20,090	$13,296
WYOMING	15,650	$ 9,870
TOTAL	7,948,560	$10,259

Sources for Trading Price Information and Research/ Analysis of the Limited Partnership Secondary Market

The following sources provide information and research/analysis on limited partnerships in the secondary market:

1. Robert A. Stanger & Company
    1129 Broad Street
    Shrewsbury, NJ 07702-4314
    908-389-3600

    Publishes *The Stanger Report,* and *Stanger's Partnership Watch.* Also publishes *Sponsor Performance Profiles.*

2. Standard & Poor's
    25 Broadway
    New York, NY 10004
    212-208-1659

    Publishes *Sponsor and Partnership Report Updates* on various limited partnership sponsors.

3. Investment Advisor
    179 Avenue of the Common
    Shrewsbury, NJ 07702
    908-389-8700

Also known as *Stanger's Investment Advisor*, became independent in 1991. Publishes partnership data and reports regularly on partnership developments.

4. Partnership Profiles, Inc.
    P.O. Box 7938
    Dallas, TX 75209

    Publishes a bimonthly *"guide through the partnership jungle"* called *The Perspective*. Also publishes the *Partnership Profiles*, a biannual review of individual partnerships.

5. Liquidity Fund
    1900 Powell Street
    7th Floor
    Emeryville, CA 94608
    800-227-4688

    Publishes research reports on various partnerships for use within selling groups. Also provides investment banking functions and specific analysis requests.

6. Disclosure, Inc.
    5161 River Rd.
    Bethesda, MD 20816
    1-800-638-8241

    Current and historical information on all public companies and LPs. 10Ks, 10Qs, prospectuses and much more. Available on demand, CD, fiche and on-line.

Trading price information on partnerships can be obtained from the following sources:

1. Stanger (see above)
2. Partnership Profiles (see above)
3. American Association of Limited Partners
    1555 Connecticut Avenue, N.W.
    Suite 308
    Washington, DC 20036
    202-797-3736
4. Investment Advisor (see above)

Sample Secondary Market Research Reports

Some secondary market firms prepare reports on selected limited partnerships. Such a report, produced by Liquidity Fund, follows.

LIQUIDITY FUND   I N V E S T M E N T   C O R P O R A T I O N

JMB INCOME PROPERTIES VIII, Ltd.

Overview

JMB Income Properties, Ltd.-VIII ("JMBVIII") is a moderately leveraged equity real estate partnership formed in 1981 to invest in income-producing commercial real estate. The Partnership originally invested in six retail properties and one office property; four retail properties remain. As has been the case with much of the real estate market in the United States, several of the properties in the portfolio have not experienced appreciation in value relative to their purchase price. Investors who acquire an interest in this partnership through the secondary market enter the Partnership in its operational phase, avoiding start-up risks, and are able to purchase units at a discount from estimated current liquidation value.

Sponsor:	JMB Realty
Offering:	1981
Gross Subscription:	$80,005,000
Original Unit Price:	$1,000
Remaining Capital:	$801.70

Estimated Break-Up Value Per Unit:	$563
Current Annualized Distribution Per Unit:	$16
* Distribution Coverage Percentage:	57%

Call Liquidity Fund Trading Desk for Current Price

(800) 548-7355

January 1992

* Coverage After Principal Payments and Capital Improvements, based on 9 months to 9/30/91, annualized.

JMBVIII currently provides annualized quarterly cash distributions of $16 per unit.

Investment Benefits

Experienced Management

Founded in 1968, JMB Realty ("JMB") is the nation's leading syndicator with over 20 years of experience in real estate investment, management and development. Privately owned by officers and employees, syndication is only one segment of JMB's primary business activities, which include property development, institutional investment management, property management and leasing, property acquisition and sales, and insurance. JMB is one of the largest equity owners of commercial real estate in North America, holding over $20 billion in real estate properties. JMB's investment strategy is to invest in quality properties with strong long-term investment potential. The success of JMB-sponsored programs over the years can be attributed in part to the sponsor's ability to effectively manage its partnership's properties in overbuilt markets and under tight credit conditions. (See, "Investment Considerations," below.)

Cash Distributions

JMBVIII currently distributes cash to its limited partners at the rate of $16 per unit per annum. (Call the Liquidity Fund Trading Desk for current prices.) (See, "Portfolio Cash Flow" for further discussion on Partnership distribution levels.)

Investment Considerations

Concentration of Portfolio Equity

Approximately sixty-five percent of current estimated portfolio equity is concentrated in two properties: 35% in the Town and Country Center and 30% in the Georgia Square Shopping Mall. Town and Country Center is located in Houston, Texas. The Houston economy is beginning to strengthen, and properties in Houston have begun to show signs of recovery and appreciation. Houston has been ranked among the ten hottest markets for real estate investment; however, investments in this market should still be made with a longer-term perspective. Georgia Square is located in Athens, Georgia, approximately 65 miles northeast of Atlanta. The property has a long record of strong occupancy, and as of September 30, 1991 was 93% leased. (See, "Key Properties".)

Portfolio Cash Flow

Limited partner distributions were covered by operational cash flow for the first nine months of 1991, as they were in 1990. However, limited partner distributions have not been covered by cash flow after principal payments and capital improvements since 1988. Particularly in 1991, capital improvements have been substantial. Specifically, capital resources have been needed to fund building improvements and tenant leasehold improvements at the Carillon Shopping Village and Georgia Square Shopping Mall. The Partnership elected to reduce its distribution level in 1990, and given the current distribution coverage level and likely continued demands on Partnership reserves, it would not be unlikely for another reduction to occur. Over the long term, a policy which limits distributions to the level of operational cash flow will work to preserve the investment potential of the Partnership's properties.

Key Properties

Georgia Square is a 680,000 square foot enclosed mall in Athens, Georgia. This property represents 21% of the Partnership's original cash investment in real estate. The Partnership, through a joint venture, owns an interest in approximately 473,000 square feet. Athens, located 65 miles northeast of Atlanta, is the home of the University of Georgia. The University is the major employer in the city. The two-level regional mall is the only enclosed shopping center in the Athens area. The property, which was originally constructed in 1981, is currently undergoing an extensive interior and minor exterior renovation. This renovation project should be completed by the end of the second quarter of 1992. Even though over half of the mall leases expired in 1991, it appears that the renovation was helpful not only in retaining existing tenants, but in attracting new ones, as the rollover did not create a vacancy problem. However, several

PROPERTY INFORMATION SUMMARY

Property/Location Square Footage	Percent of Current Estimated Equity	Occupancy as of 9/30/91
RETAIL		
Town & Country Center Houston, TX		
1,054,000 sq. ft.	35%	60%
Georgia Square Athens, GA		
680,000 sq. ft.	30%	93%
Clackamas Town Center Portland, OR		
1,209,000 sq. ft.	20%	99%
Carillon Houston, TX		
182,000 sq. ft.	15%	66%

of the new leases required significant tenant improvements which will substantially affect Partnership cash flow. Two of the anchor tenants, Davidson's and Sears, own their own stores. Other anchors include Belk Department Store, J.C. Penney and General Cinema. In 1989, a smaller retail center, Perimeter Square, was built across the street from Georgia Square. Perimeter Square is anchored by Wal-Mart, Phar-Mor Drugs and the Food Lion. This property has not affected the Partnership's property because of its dissimilar tenant profile. Georgia Square has had a very strong historical occupancy level of over 98%. Occupancy at the end of the third quarter of 1991 was 93%.

Town & Country Center in Houston, Texas represents 39% of the Partnership's original cash invested in real estate. The regional shopping center, which was built in 1983, contains 1,054,000 square feet of space, six free standing buildings and a three-level enclosed mall area. The first and second floors have consistently enjoyed high occupancy levels; however, the third floor continues to experience vacancy problems. Anchors which are attached to the mall and own their own stores are Dillard's, Neiman-Marcus, Marshall Field and J.C. Penney. The Partnership, through a joint venture, holds an interest in 370,000 square feet of the mall space. Principal tenants in the mall space owned by the partnership are The Gap and Luby's Cafeteria. Occupancy at the end of the third quarter of 1991 was 60%. This property is prominently located adjacent to a recently-completed freeway exit off of the "loop" around the city of Houston. This improved access has greatly increased traffic to the Center. Over the past year there have been indications that the Houston economy is beginning to strengthen and diversify away from its strong dependence on the oil sector. This diversification should help to stabilize the economy and increase absorption of retail space. While properties in Houston are beginning to show signs of recovery and appreciation, investments in this market should be made with a longer-term perspective.

Clackamas Town Center, located in Clackamas County (Portland), Oregon, represents 10% of the Partnership's original cash investment in real estate. The 1,209,000 square foot, two-level enclosed regional mall has been very successful, and due to its strength and stability, it is expected to continue to perform well. Clackamas Town Center is located in the center of the largest concentration of retail space in the state of Oregon. Anchors who own their own space are Meier & Frank, Montgomery Ward, J.C. Penney, Sears and Nordstrom. Occupancy at the end of the third quarter 1991 was 99%. JMB is exploring the possibility of selling the Partnership's interest in this property.

Carillon West Shopping Village is a 182,000 square foot specialty shopping center in Houston, Texas. This investment represents 10% of the Partnership's original cash invested in real estate and 15% of current estimated equity. The property is a two-story center with an excellent location on one of the area's busiest streets. The tenant mix is primarily entertainment and food oriented, with Wyatt's Cafeteria and the Great Caruso Restaurant as major tenants. Occupancy at the end of the third quarter of 1991 stood at 66%.

Financial Summary	1991*	1990	1989
Operating Cash Flow	$46.14	$39.63	26.63
Cash Flow After Principal Payments & Capital Improvements	$ 9.09	$25.65	$16.91
Limited Partner Distributions	$16.00	$32.10	$48.20
Distribution Coverage Percentage (After PP & CI)	57%	80%	35%
Net Current Assets	$44.35	$51.21	$54.68

*The first nine months of 1991 annualized.

HUTTON/CONAM REALTY INVESTORS 4

Overview

Hutton/ConAm Realty Investors 4 ("HC4") is a low-leverage real estate limited partnership which is invested solely in apartment properties. Each property is a modern apartment community with excellent appreciation potential. The high quality of these properties is demonstrated by their ability to continually attract upscale tenants relative to other apartment complexes in their areas.

Secondary market investors, unlike the original investors, avoid some of the inherent risks and pitfalls of investing in the primary issue of the partnership, such as offering fees/expenses and the lack of track record inherent in blind pools. Further-

General Partner:	ConAm Services
Offering:	1984-1987
Gross Subscription:	$64,055,000
Original Unit Price:	$500
Remaining Capital:	$500

Estimated Break -Up Value Per Unit:	$278
Current Annualized Distribution Per Unit:	$21.20
Distribution Coverage Percentage:	96%
Portfolio Leverage:	12%

Call Liquidity Fund Trading Desk for Current Price

(800) 548-7355

February, 1992

more, an investor in the secondary market is typically able to purchase the units at a substantial discount to estimated liquidation value. This has the effect of locking in appreciation and capital gains, even if the portfolio value remains flat. HC4 currently provides annualized quarterly cash distributions of $21.20 per unit. Thus, HC4 provides an attractive investment opportunity for investors desiring a quality apartment property portfolio with modest leverage and good appreciation potential.

Investment Benefits

Apartment Concentration

HC4's real estate portfolio consists exclusively of apartments. We feel apartments are particularly attractive as the real estate recovery is clearly underway in this sector. In the two year period 1989-1990, prices of high quality apartments nationwide rose 7.8%, while apartment rents during the same period rose 8.5%, according to the National Real Estate Index. This improvement is largely attributable to the fact that apartments were the first property type to experience a dramatic decline in construction. In 1990, approximately 252,000 multi-family units were permitted for construction, 62% below the 656,000 units permitted in the peak year 1985. This decrease was partially due to the restrictive lending practices of most banks and insurance companies which, in the short term, could hamper the Partnership's ability to sell or refinance the properties (see **Investment Considerations**). In the long run, however, this will allow HC4 to increase rents and ensure a stable asset value and income stream for the Partnership. HC4's portfolio of apartments has been, and will continue to be, positively affected by these decreases in construction, especially in Florida where

new construction in some cases is down over 90% from peak year levels. In fact, HC4's General Partner was able to raise the rent on all their Florida properties in late 1990 for the first time in several years.

Management Expertise

HC4 is co-managed by Hutton Real Estate Services ("Hutton") and ConAm Property Services ("ConAm"). Although Hutton arranged the fund raising and continues to provide the administrative needs of the partnership, ConAm plays the most integral role in the future success of the portfolio. ConAm handled the property selection and acquisition and currently administers all property management for the Partnership. ConAm, based in San Diego, has considerable experience in property management, currently managing over $1.5 billion in property. Most of these properties are part of the 50 public and private real estate limited partnerships sponsored or co-sponsored by ConAm since the early 1970's.

Investment Considerations

Short-Term Outlook

Demand has been flat due to the recession, resulting in no income growth. Also affecting property value is the drastically reduced activity in the financing market which has created little opportunity for sales or refinancings. However, the ongoing decline in new construction, coupled with the signs of an economic recovery, should eventually increase demand which will put upward pressure on rents and push values higher.

Distribution Security

The key to maintaining the HC4 distribution is keeping the properties well maintained and fully occupied. Portions of future cash flow may be required for capital improvements to ensure continued high occupancy levels. This may result in slightly less cash available for distribution to the limited partners.

In 1990 and through the 3rd quarter of 1991 cash distributions to the limited partners slightly exceeded the net cash flow generated by the properties. While HC4 holds a large amount of cash in reserve, unless property operations improve, this reserve will be slowly depleted over time if the current distribution policy continues. (See "Distribution Coverage Percentage" on the Financial Summary)

Diversification

HC4's portfolio is over 70% concentrated in Florida, based on estimated limited partnership equity. If Florida does not participate in the projected recovery of the nationwide apartment market, there may be a negative effect on the performance of the partnership's portfolio. Fortunately, Florida's economy has only suffered slightly from the current national recession, and according to a recent forecast by the WEFA Group (formerly Wharton Econometrics), ranks well above the national average in projected population and employment growth during the 1990's.

PROPERTY INFORMATION SUMMARY

Property/Location Number of Units	Percent of Current Estimated Equity	Occupancy as of 9/30/91
The Trails at Meadowlakes Deerfield Beach, FL 189 Units	10%	94%
Pelican Landing Clearwater, FL 204 Units	25%	93%
Village at the Foothills II Tucson, AZ 120 Units	10%	93%
River Hill Apartments Irving, TX 192 Apartments	19%	93%
Shadowood Village Jacksonville, FL 110 Units	12%	94%
Cypress Lake Apartments Fort Lauderdale, FL 176 Units	24%	88%

Properties

Cypress Lakes Apartments, built in 1987, is located in Fort Lauderdale, Florida overlooking the private ten-acre lake for which the property is named. The property boasts lake views from each apartment and includes such amenities as a pool, jacuzzi, washers and dryers in each unit, and a clubhouse. Fort Lauderdale has suffered from overbuilding like much of the country and consequently, rents have remained flat over the past few years. However, the number of new units built in the area has declined each year since 1984 while absorption has remained stable. In fact, during the first quarter of 1991, fewer than 200 multi-family units were permitted for construction in Broward county, down over 90% from the first quarter 1990. This dramatic decrease in construction should keep occupancy strong and in time, lead to higher rents and a higher property value.

Pelican Landing, built in 1985, is located in Clearwater, Florida, a suburb of Tampa. The property has considerable amenities including a lighted tennis court, a pool with jacuzzi, sauna, and clubhouse. The property consists solely of two bedroom units. Just as in Broward Co., the local multifamily market has tightened up recently as the number of new units coming on line has dropped significantly. Rents should continue to rise as the effect of this slower building positively affects supply.

River Hill Apartments, built in 1985, is located in Los Colinas, Texas, a 12,000 acre planned community twelve miles outside Dallas. The property is well situated with respect to schools, recreational facilities, and employment opportunities in Dallas. Specifically, the project is composed of approximately twenty-one two and three story clusters. Each unit includes a fireplace, a washer and dryer hookup, a trash compactor, and access to a swimming pool and clubhouse.
Also, the project is surrounded by security fencing and has restricted entrance. The Dallas area, especially the northern part where Los Colinas is located, has shown tremendous improvement in the multifamily market. The local occupancy average is in the high 90% and rents have started to rise for the first time since the mid 1980's.

Shadowood Village, built in 1986, is one part of a three-apartment community known as "Villages at Creekside" located in Jacksonville, Florida. The other two properties are owned by affiliated partnerships. Although this property may be sold separately, it has the potential, when combined with the other two properties, to attract an institutional investor's interest. Jacksonville's multifamily housing market is rapidly improving. Rents were up over five percent in 1990, mainly attributable to a substantial decline in construction and continuing strong demand for housing in this area. In fact, Fortune recently voted Jacksonville the ninth best city for business, which may help explain why AT&T Universal Card Services, Merrill Lynch Equity Management, Tandem Financial Group, and Lamborgini all relocated their operations to Jacksonville during 1990.

The Trails at Meadow Lakes, built in 1985, is located in Deerfield Beach, Florida, just outside of Fort Lauderdale. It is the only property in the portfolio subject to a mortgage (loan to estimated value ratio= 58%). The property was originally purchased using all cash but subsequently financed in order to help fund the purchase of Cypress Lakes, also located in the Fort Lauderdale area. This property has continuously maintained high occupancy levels which is attributable to the tightening market (see "Clearwater Lake" summary), and the above average quality of the complex.

Village at the Foothills II, built in 1985, is the second phase of a project located in the premier part of Tucson. Its excellent location and recent construction help make it one of the better apartment buildings in Tucson. This, combined with a full offering of amenities, including fireplaces, wet bars, washers and dryers, and access to a pool and tennis courts, have kept rents and occupancy very high, relative to other properties in the market. Although the Tucson market remains overbuilt, it too is benefiting from the decline in construction and, considering its strong population growth rate, should participate in the multi-family recovery.

Financial Summary (per unit)

	1990	1989	1988
Cash Flow After Principal Payments & Capital Improvements	$20.31	$21.54	$17.94
Limited Partner Distributions	$21.20	$21.20	$16.95
Distribution Coverage Percentage	96%	102%	106%
Net Current Assets	$13.10	$18.38	$18.69

APPENDIX F

Partnership Rollup Market Statistics

FIGURE F1 Rollup Performance

Comparison of Exchange Value and Closing Prices
1st Day, 30 Days, 90 Days†, Current (12/31/91)

	Exchange	Symbol	# Investors	First Trade Date	Exchange Value $ (per Unit)	First Day Close $	First Day Close % Change	30 Day Close $	30 Day Close % Change	90 Day Close $	90 Day Close % Change	Current Performance as of 12/31/91 $	Current Performance as of 12/31/91 % Change
Real Estate Roll-Ups													
American Real Estate Partners	NYSE	ACP	30,000	7/23/87	20.00	16.38	-18.1%	16.13	-19.4%	14.25	-28.8%	9.75	-51.3%
Centennial Group, Inc.	ASE	CEQ	27,000	6/26/87	10.00	6.88	-31.2%	6.13	-38.8%	5.88	-41.2%	0.13	-98.8%
Halwood Realty Partners††	ASE	HRY	87,000	11/2/90	30.00	6.50	-78.3%	5.75	-80.8%	4.50	-85.0%	2.00	-93.3%
IRE/Bank Atlantic Debentures	OTC	.	8,300	6/1/89	50.00	24.00	-52.0%	20.00	-60.0%	18.00	-64.0%	10.00*	-80.0%
National Realty, L.P.	ASE	NLP	46,000	10/6/87	200.00	80.00	-60.0%	80.00	-60.0%	67.50	-66.3%	12.00	-94.0%
Southwest Realty	ASE	SWL	4,400	2/9/83	20.00**	13.60	-32.0%	13.35	-33.3%	13.40	-33.0%	0.94	-95.3%
Milestone Properties, Inc.	NYSE	MPI	6,300	1/30/91	13.83***	3.87	-72.0%	3.73	-73.0%	4.13	-70.2%	2.50	-81.9%
United Realty Group L.P.	OTC	URLPZ	2,500	5/6/91	15.00	4.50	-70.0%	1.38	-90.8%	1.00	-93.3%	0.25*	-98.3%
Berkshire Realty Company Inc.	NYSE	BRI	15,700	6/29/91	15.00	8.88	-40.8%	10.13	-32.5%	8.88	-40.8%	8.63	-42.5%
Average Decline Real Estate Roll-Ups							-50.5%		-54.3%		-58.1%		-81.7%
Oil/Gas Roll-Ups													
Callon Consolidated Partners LP	OTC	CCLPZ	18,900	12/19/88	10.00	2.50	-75.0%	3.25	-67.5%	3.50	-65.0%	1.38*	-86.3%
Kelley Oil & Gas Partners	ASE	KLY	12,100	1/24/86	20.00	12.13	-39.4%	11.50	-42.5%	9.75	-51.3%	14.00	-30.0%
Samson Energy Co., LP	ASE	SAM	3,000	1/16/86	20.00	15.13	-24.4%	13.88	-30.6%	15.63	-21.9%	11.88	-40.6%
Mission Resource Partners LP	ASE	MRP	4,000	4/18/88	10.00	9.13	-8.7%	6.63	-33.7%	6.63	-33.7%	§	§
Parker & Parsley Development LP	ASE	PDP	6,500	12/22/87	20.00	14.00	-30.0%	17.13	-14.4%	15.63	-21.9%	§	§
Average Decline Oil/Gas Roll-Ups							-35.5%		-36.0%		-38.7%		-52.3%
Equipment Leasing Roll-Ups													
PLM International Inc.	ASE	PLM	23,700	2/3/88	15.00	8.38	-44.1%	7.38	-50.8%	8.25	-45.0%	3.00	-80.0%
Total # Investors			295,400										
Average Decline All Roll-Ups							-45.1%		-48.0%		-50.7%		-74.8%

NOTE: This is an analysis of all roll-ups/restructurings completed to date which included substantially all non-traded partnerships converted to a currently traded entity.
* Approximation of trading level of BankAtlantic debentures; share prices for United Realty Group and Callon Consolidated Partners were unavailable for 12/31/91 and so are current (1/9/92).
** Includes price of Southwest Realty warrants issued in exchange offer (one warrant for every 5 shares issued).
*** Share prices are blended to arrive at one share price for both common and preferred stock issued in the exchange.
§ Current share prices are not stated for Parker & Parsley and Mission Resource Partners. These entities recently underwent restructurings which exclude their securities from tracking.
† 30 and 90 day closing prices are based on calendar days rather than working days (if date falls on a weekend or holiday, price used is the next day's price).
†† Halwood Realty was haircut 50% from appraised value to arrive at exchange value. Exchange value noted here represents actual appraisal value before 50% haircut. "90 Day Close" represents 2/4/91 close price.
INFORMATION SOURCES: ROBERT STANGER, OFFERING PROSPECTUS, AND STANDARD & POOR'S DAILY STOCK PRICE RECORDS
15-Apr-92

GLOSSARY

accredited investor As defined by the SEC, an investor in a private limited partnership who has a net worth of at least $1 million, or an annual income of at least $200,000, or a net worth that is at least five times as much as his or her interest in the partnership and said interest is at least $150,000.

acquisition fees The total of all fees and commissions paid to affiliates or nonaffiliates in connection with the purchase of a property for a real estate investment program, including real estate commissions, development fees, selection fees and nonrecurring management fees, but not including loan fees (points) paid for mortgage brokerage services.

adjusted basis Price upon which capital gains or losses are calculated when an asset is sold. For example, the sales price of property is adjusted for depreciation.

alternative minimum tax (AMT) A federal income tax intended to ensure that individuals, trusts and estates that benefit from tax preferences do not escape all federal tax liability.

basis The cost and out-of-pocket expenses (e.g., commission) of acquiring an investment asset. When the investor sells the asset, the basis is subtracted from the sales price to determine the capital gain or loss.

bid price The highest price a prospective buyer is prepared to pay to acquire a security or asset.

blind pool program   An investment program that at the time of inception does not have the proceeds of the offering allocated to specific projects or properties.

blue-sky laws   A popular name for laws enacted by various states to protect the public against securities frauds. The term is believed to have originated when a judge ruled that a particular stock had about the same value as a patch of blue sky.

book value   In accounting, the cost of an asset minus its accumulated depreciation.

break-up value   The actual per-unit present cash value of a limited partnership, assuming all assets are sold at current market rates, all liabilities paid off, any partnership joint venture or sharing arrangements are fulfilled, and remaining cash is paid out according to the partnership agreement.

broker   In securities, a person who serves as the intermediary between a buyer and a seller, usually receiving a commission for each completed transaction.

broker-dealer   A firm that has fulfilled various state and federal securities regulations and is licensed to buy and sell securities.

capitalization rate (cap rate)   An approach to evaluating the sales price of income property based on its current net operating income, exclusive of mortgage or financing expenses.

cash flow   An analysis of the changes in a cash account during a given period, such as a month, quarter or year. If cash income exceeds cash expenses, the cash flow is positive; in the opposite case, cash flow is negative.

closing costs   The expenses involved in transferring the title of real property, including the costs of title search, title insurance and filing fees.

commission   Fee charged by a broker for executing the purchase or sale of securities or the sale of property.

dealer   In securities, an individual or company trading for its own account.

depreciation   In tax accounting, the deduction for the amortization of the cost of fixed assets over their useful life, even though the assets may be appreciating in value. Land is not depreciable, but improvements, structures and equipment are.

development loan A mortgage loan to finance all or part of the cost of acquiring and developing land.

discount Reduction in price in exchange for quick cash payment.

distribution Payment made from a partnership to its limited partners. Since a distribution may include return of capital in addition to operating income, it should not be confused with "yield," which refers exclusively to operating income received from invested capital.

equity An owner's interest in a property or business; the market value of the property or business, less all claims and liens upon it.

equity REIT A real estate investment trust (REIT) that acquires income-producing properties, as contrasted with a mortgage REIT, which makes or purchases loans on real estate.

foreclosure A legal process whereby the mortgagee takes possession of the property when the mortgagor defaults on payments. The property is usually sold at a court-administered auction, with the proceeds assigned to the mortgagee to pay off the balance due; any remaining proceeds go to the former owner.

front-end fees A sales charge or organizational fees incurred on the purchase of an investment.

general partner An individual who is personally responsible for the activities and management of a partnership and has full personal liability for its debts and obligations.

gross multiplier In real estate, a method of evaluating property using an analysis of the property's income compared to that of similar properties in the same or comparable market area.

illiquid A security that does not have an active secondary market and is therefore difficult to convert to cash before maturity.

invested capital Capital contributions of investors in a limited partnership, less the sum of cumulative surplus funds distributed to investors.

joint venture A form of business organized by two or more persons or companies to carry out an enterprise for profit. Joint venturers share in the project's management, profits and losses, and liabilities.

lease A contract between a property owner and tenant setting forth conditions upon which a tenant may occupy and use property.

leverage In investments, the investor's use of borrowed money, such as the purchase of stocks on margin or the securing of a mortgage to finance the purchase of income-producing real estate.

liability Any claim against assets, such as debts, liens or mortgages.

lien A claim against a property that has been pledged or mortgaged to secure the performance of an obligation.

limited partnership A business entity formed by one or more general partners (individuals or corporations) and one or more limited partners. General partners are personally responsible for management of the business and are personally liable for its debts and obligations. Limited partners contribute cash or property to finance the business, but are not responsible for management nor personally liable for the partnership's debts and obligations. The limited partnership agreement describes all the rights, powers and duties of the partners, including fees the general partners will receive, the distribution of profits, income, tax advantages, the transferability of interest in the partnership and the like.

liquid asset Cash or a marketable security easily converted to cash.

liquidation In general, the process of converting securities or other property to cash.

liquidity The ability of the market in a particular security or commodity to absorb a reasonable amount of buying or selling at reasonable price changes. Or, the ability of an individual or company to convert assets to cash without a significant loss of value.

markup When a broker buys a security on behalf of a client, the markup is the difference between the purchase price and the price at which it is sold to the client (see spread).

market maker A dealer willing to quote prices and transact orders at any time for the purchase or sale of given securities.

market value In general, the price at which a wiling seller would sell and a willing buyer would buy, neither being under any compulsion. In securities, the price at which the most recent trade was executed. In real estate, an estimate of the highest bid a property would elicit on the open market from an intelligent and informed buyer.

mortgage An instrument by which a borrower gives a lender a legally valid and enforceable claim (lien) against property pledged as security for a loan. The borrower continues to have use of the property; when the loan is repaid, the lien is removed. If the borrower defaults on his or her payments, the lender may petition the court to seize and auction the property (foreclosure) and allocate the proceeds to pay off the loan.

mortgage REIT A real estate investment trust (REIT) that specialized in either making or buying permanent mortgage loans or providing interim or long-term financing for construction and development projects.

National Association of Securities Dealers (NASD) A nonprofit self-regulatory association of brokers and dealers in the over-the-counter securities business, under the supervision of the Securities and Exchange Commission. The NASD maintains and enforces professional and ethical standards and procedures for securities trading and licenses securities professionals.

NASDAQ The NASD Automated Quotations system for providing brokers and dealers with price quotations.

net asset value (NAV) The market price of all assets owned minus liabilities.

net operating income In real estate, the income from improved real property, including the land, buildings and other improvements, after operating expenses (taxes, insurance, utilities, maintenance, etc.,—exclusive of mortgage or finance expenses).

new issue   The initial offering of a stock, bond or partnership.

occupancy rate   In real estate, the percentage of an income property that is leased on a given date. For multifamily housing, the number of rent-paying units divided by the number of rentable units; for commercial and industrial properties, the number of square feet leased divided by the number of leasable square feet.

offer   The price at which a person who owns an asset or security is ready to sell.

oil and gas limited partnership   A limited partnership organized to finance the drilling, completion or operation of oil and gas wells.

over-the-counter (OTC) market   Market for trading securities that are not listed on the organized stock exchanges. Transactions are conducted through NASDAQ, a telephone and computer network administered by the National Association of Securities Dealers (NASD).

partnership   A contract of two or more persons to unite their property, labor, skill or some combination or them, in prosecution of some joint business, and to share the profits and liabilities in certain proportions.

phantom income   Taxable income in excess of cash income received. This arises in an investment program, for example, when the actual cash distributions to investors are less than the program's reportable income as proportionally assigned to each investor.

phantom gain   Taxable capital gains in excess of cash gains received. This arises when a secondary market purchaser of limited partnership interests assumes the basis of the original owner and that basis is less than the actual capital invested by the new owner.

portfolio   Holding of diverse securities or assets.

principal   (1) A dealer buying or selling for his own account or the person for whom a broker executes an order; (2) investment capital, exclusive of earnings; and (3) the face amount of a debt instrument.

private limited partnership A limited partnership whose offering is not registered with the Securities and Exchange Commission, under an exemption granted in the Securities Act of 1933. Shares or units in the partnership are sold by investment advisors, financial planners and brokerage firms to investors who meet financial suitability requirements for income and net worth.

private placement The sale of securities or private limited partnership units directly to a limited number of investors. Such offerings need not be registered with the Securities and Exchange Commission. Also known as Reg D offering.

prospectus The document that offers a new issue of securities, mutual funds or limited partnerships to the public. The prospectus provides all the information an investor needs to make an educated decision about the offering.

public limited partnership A limited partnership that is registered with the Securities and Exchange Commission and distributed in a public offering by broker-dealers or employees of the sponsor.

quotation, quote The highest bid to buy and the lowest offer to sell a security in a given market at a given time.

quoted price The last price at which the sale and purchase of a security or commodity was made.

real estate investment trust (REIT) A company that invests in equity (equity REIT) or mortgages (mortgage REIT) on all types of properties, and offers shares that are publicly traded.

registered representative An employee of a member firm of an exchange or of a broker-dealer who has met the requirements of an exchange as to background and knowledge of the securities business; acts as a customer's broker and is compensated on a commission basis. Also known as an account executive or broker in a NYSE firm. Financial planners are also registered representatives on the NASD.

Regulation D The Securities and Exchange Commission regulation that defines an accredited investor in a private limited partnership.

Reg D offering The sale of securities or private limited partnership units directly to a limited number of investors. Such offerings need not be registered with the Securities and Exchange Commission. Also known as private placement.

return The pretax profit on an investment, expressed as an annual percentage of the investor's original capital; the sum of the net change in the investment's market value and any dividends or interest paid divided by the purchase price.

return of capital A distribution to an investor from a source other than net income as determined for tax or accounting purposes. A return of capital is not taxable.

rollup A controversial practice of "rolling up" a number of limited partnerships into a single security. Thousands of investors have lost millions of dollars in partnership rollups (see Appendix F).

safe harbor Provision in a law, rule or regulation that excuses a business entity from liability for noncompliance under certain stated conditions.

seasoned security A high-quality issue that has demonstrated liquidity in the secondary market.

secondary market Market in which securities are bought and sold subsequent to their original issue; the original issuer does not participate in the trading or its proceeds. Stock exchanges and over-the-counter markets are secondary markets.

Securities and Exchange Commission (SEC) A federal regulatory and enforcement agency that oversees public investment trading activities by facilitating fair and orderly securities markets, enforcing statutory corporate disclosure requirements, and regulating investment companies, investment advisers and public utility holding companies.

Section 754 election An adjustment a general partner can make in the partnership's accounting that allows new purchasers of units in the secondary market to have a new tax basis instead of assuming the basis of the original limited partner.

self-liquidating program An investment vehicle that from its inception provides for liquidation and distribution of assets at a future date; a limited partnership whose organizational documents provide for a limited life.

sponsor Any person instrumental in organizing and managing a limited partnership; a general partner.

spread The difference between the price at which a dealer buys a security or partnership unit for its own account and the price at which it is later sold.

stock exchange An organization registered under the Securities Exchange Act of 1934 that offers physical facilities for member brokers and dealers to buy and sell securities in a two-way auction.

subordinated incentive fee Compensation to the general partners of a limited partnership as an added incentive for profitable operations. The partnership agreement specifies performance standards to be achieved in order for the fee to be earned.

suitability rules Rules of professional practice that require brokers and dealers to have reasonable grounds for believing that a customer's financial means are adequate to assume the risks involved in speculative investments.

tax basis The original cost of an asset if purchased, or the fair market value of that asset if inherited, less accumulated depreciation.

tax shelter An investment that lowers a taxpayer's current tax liability by providing deductions against taxable income.

yield In general, the amount of profit of an investment of capital.

INDEX